Accountability and Privacy in Network Security

Yuxiang Ma · Yulei Wu · Jingguo Ge

Accountability and Privacy in Network Security

Yuxiang Ma
Henan University
Kaifeng, Henan, China

Yulei Wu (ID)
University of Exeter
Exeter, UK

Jingguo Ge
Institute of Information Engineering
Chinese Academy of Sciences
Beijing, Beijing, China

ISBN 978-981-15-6574-8   ISBN 978-981-15-6575-5   (eBook)
https://doi.org/10.1007/978-981-15-6575-5

This Springer imprint is published by the registered company Springer Nature Singapore Pte Ltd.
The registered company address is: 152 Beach Road, #21-01/04 Gateway East, Singapore 189721,
Singapore

Preface

Since its birth, the Internet has profoundly changed human society. It connects people to people, people to things, and things to things. In the network, people can obtain content located at any nodes and use resources that may not be available locally. The Internet helps people to complete work more efficiently. In addition, people use the network to connect with friends or expand social circle. With the fast development of network technologies, the network constantly brings people new surprises. The benefits of the Internet have exceeded people's initial expectations.

While the network brings convenience to human lives, various problems of the network are being gradually surfaced, such as the lack of IP addresses, insufficient support for mobility, and a series of security issues. Among them, people concern about the security of the network significantly. Numerous research has focused on network security, and the public news about network security usually attracts more wide discussions. Security is an important foundation of the network, and it is related to the vital interests of every user. If a network is clearly insecure, the motivation of using that network will be directly affected. When people notice that their privacy is at risk of being leaked, they manage to use encryption technologies and even some well-known tools, e.g., Tor, to strengthen the protection of their privacy. The leakage and misuse of users' private information can lead to many negative results. However, uncontrolled privacy protection schemes breed criminal issues and affect the legitimate rights and interests of users. Network attackers may use powerful privacy protection schemes to avoid being discovered and monitored, threatening the safety of normal network users. Therefore, unlimited privacy protection is not conducive to the development of the network. The privacy protection and behavior accountability are two important factors of network security. The ideal condition is to find a balance between them, which is the focus of this book.

The first reaction when people see the words privacy and accountability is that they are a set of opposite needs. If people want to protect the identity of users in the network, it is difficult to achieve accountability. An extreme case is complete anonymity. If people want to emphasize accountability, it is difficult to protect the privacy of users, since obtaining user identity is necessary for accountability. If we cannot grasp the identifier of a user, how can we determine who should be responsible for malicious behaviors? Because of this contradiction, there exist many challenges for achieving a balance between privacy protection and behavior accountability.

In this book, the research related to accountability and privacy in the network is introduced. There are eight chapters in this book. The goal of each chapter and the relationship between chapters are presented as follows.

In Chap. 1, the main content of this book is introduced. The definitions of privacy and accountability are provided from the view of network users and network managers (e.g., Internet Service Providers and governments).

In Chap. 2, the studies related to accountability and privacy are reviewed, as well as new network architectures and emerging network technologies which we use in the field of privacy and accountability.

In Chap. 3, a neural network method for encrypted traffic classification is proposed. This chapter confirms that it is not enough to use encryption technologies to protect the user privacy. In the proposed method, when given a network traffic flow, we can figure out whether it is encrypted, and identify which application class (such as P2P and VoIP) it belongs to. Then, we can speculate on the user's behavior and obtain the privacy of a user.

In Chaps. 4, 5, and 6, we propose the architectures that can balance privacy and accountability in the network. These architectures are content-based, flow-based, and service-based, respectively. In Chap. 7, an architecture for accountable anonymous access in Named Data Networking (NDN) is proposed to address the lack of accountability on user behavior in NDN. Finally, we introduce future directions and conclude the study in Chap. 8.

This book discusses accountability and privacy in network security from a technical perspective, providing a comprehensive overview of the state-of-the-art research, as well as the current challenges and open issues. Further, it proposes a set of new and innovative solutions to balance the privacy and the accountability in the network, in terms of content, flow and service, focusing on the application of new technologies and new concepts of networks. The solutions take into consideration key components (e.g., in-network cache) learned from future network architectures, and adopt the emerging blockchain technique to ensure the security and scalability of the proposed architectures. In addition, the book examines in detail the related studies on accountability and privacy, and validates the architectures using real-world datasets. This book presents secure, scalable solutions that can detect malicious behaviors in the network in a timely manner without compromising user privacy.

This book is a valuable resource for undergraduate and postgraduate students, researchers and engineers working in the fields of network architecture and cybersecurity. Graduate students can select promising research topics from this book that are suitable for their thesis or dissertation research. Researchers will have a deep understanding of the challenging issues and opportunities for privacy and accountability. Industry engineers from IT companies, service providers, content providers, network operators, equipment manufacturers can get to know the engineering design issues and corresponding solutions after reading the discussions of real-world deployment described in chapters.

Thank you for reading this book. We wish that this book can help you with the scientific research and practical problems of network security.

Kaifeng, China

Exeter, UK

Beijing, China

Yuxiang Ma

Yulei Wu

Jingguo Ge

Contents

Chapter 1
Introduction

This chapter introduces the research background of this book and provides definitions of privacy and accountability that apply to this book. It discusses the privacy protection and behavior accountability from the perspective of different parties of a network, e.g., network users and network managers.

1.1 Background

Network users always try to hide their true identity (e.g., IP address) to protect their privacy in cyberspace [1–3]. This is because many websites collect, store and share a large amount of personal data regardless of the user's disapproval [4–6]. The current Internet allows some legitimate anonymous usages, e.g., visiting shopping websites, anonymous donations, elections or voting and anonymous reporting. In these scenarios, the user's identity information needs to be effectively protected. Currently, there are some popular technologies or protocols such as Tor, Crowds and Address Hiding Protocol (AHP) [7–9] that provide users a means to use the network anonymously. However, this anonymity conflicts with the expectations of service providers (SPs) or content providers (CPs), and, even the agreement in the cyberspace community—"one needs to be held accountable for one's actions" [1]. In addition, we should also think about whether this untrackable anonymity that can evade responsibility is what we really need.

As we all know, accountability is one of the key issues that concerns SPs and CPs most. When malicious behavior occurs in the network, network managers and victims need to know who (which node) should be punished. Therefore, Internet service providers (ISPs) need to have some information (e.g., obtaining the packet source address) to stop in-progress attacks and prevent future harmful actions [1, 10].

Y. Ma et al., *Accountability and Privacy in Network Security*, https://doi.org/10.1007/978-981-15-6575-5_1

In summary, privacy protection and behavior accountability are two critical factors in ensuring network security. At the same time, privacy and accountability are a set of conflicting needs. The existing IP source address acting as both the sender address and the return address triggers a series of contradictions between privacy and accountability [11, 12]. How to achieve both the privacy and the accountability in the network has been a challenging task.

1.2 Definition

In this book, the definitions of privacy and accountability are given below, which are consistent with many existing studies [1, 2, 4, 13–17].

Definition 1.1 Privacy protection is to ensure that when users send packets out, intermediate nodes (e.g., routers) cannot judge who is the sender according to the received packets.

Definition 1.2 Accountability refers that when malicious behaviors happen, we can find out the sender who should be responsible for the behavior.

In general, implementing accountability in the network means that the network is recordable and traceable, therefore making it liable to those communication principles for its actions [16, 17]. In other words, this refers to the ability to make network users responsible for their actions. Together with some suitable punishments or laws in the real world, it will prevent a number of attacks from being mounted [14]. In addition, accountability can raise the level of trust (in the network), i.e., trust can be addressed from the perspective of accountability [15].

It is worth noting that the security of data transmission has traditionally been entrusted to key-based cryptographic techniques. However, data encryption can only protect content from being known, but cannot effectively protect the identity of the communication entity. Therefore, research is needed to prevent intermediate routers or attackers from knowing who is communicating with others.

1.3 User's View About Privacy

It is no secret that companies like Facebook and Google collect personal information to advertise to users. However, how do people care about their privacy? A survey that was published by the Pew Research Center, conducted in the United States shows that contrary to the assertion that people do not care about privacy in the digital age, Americans have strong demands for controlling personal information and being unmonitored in their daily lives [18]. In this survey, almost all American adults (93% of adults surveyed) believed that controlling who can collect information is an important aspect of privacy protection. In the same survey, 88% of those interviewed said they did not want to be observed without approval.

In another survey report published by the Pew Research Center, we can learn that a majority of Americans (64%) believe that they have personally experienced a major data breach [19]. Although people hope that they have not been observed, they still find it difficult to avoid being monitored. It is widely believed that privacy is important to everyone, and the ability to protect the privacy of users is a long-term concern.

1.4 Manager's View About Accountability

Crimes including attacks, fraud, extortion, and theft exist in the network. With the rapid development of networking technologies, especially the continuous construction and improvement of communication infrastructure, an increasing number of users can easily access the Internet, making network security face more complex challenges. On the one hand, criminals can carry out malicious acts through convenient network access. On the other hand, the scope of being affected by malicious behaviors will be more extensive, so that more people may be affected in cyber attacks. Network management organizations, including ISPs and governments, hope to effectively monitor the user behaviors in the network. As we know, there are many illegal trading attempts to bypass regulation. A network form called "dark net" exists in the world and has a certain negative impact on the security of human society [20, 21]. Therefore, it is necessary to consider the reasonable needs for network managers to monitor the network. Because an auditable and accountable network is conducive to the healthy and long-term development of the Internet. People need a safer cyberspace environment.

The essence of finding a malicious user is by judging the source of a data packet with the malicious behavior. Therefore, if we need to achieve accountability in the network, we need to obtain the behavior of a user. However, do all the behaviors of users in the network need to be monitored in real time? Should we only need to get the user's information through specific steps when necessary (e.g., when malicious behavior occurs)? In addition, the identity and behavior of users should be mastered by special organizations, instead of allowing anyone to easily access the behaviors of other network users.

1.5 Division of Communication Modes

With the fast development of the Internet technologies, the actual needs of users and the application models of the Internet have changed greatly. The Internet is facing new challenges. For example, instead of traditional point-to-point communications, according to a white paper published by Cisco, content requesting has become a

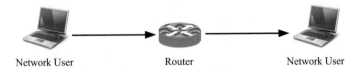

Network User   Router   Network User

Fig. 1.1 The overview of the one-to-one communication mode

major requirement for Internet users. In addition, the traffic from wireless and mobile devices will account for 71% of total IP traffic by 2022 [22], meaning that mobile communications will play a more important role in the future. In recent years, the widespread applications of emerging technologies such as big data, data mining and artificial intelligence have also brought new challenges for solving the problems of privacy protection and behavior accountability in the network [23]. Therefore, we need to consider these new requirements and new challenges when we design network solutions.

With the rapid growth of Internet traffic, the traffic characteristics at the packet level are notoriously complex and extremely variable [24–26]. Therefore, we can consider designing new schemes at alternative levels. For example, by aggregating data packets that belong to the same network flow, we can achieve the corresponding goal of that flow at the flow level. In addition, by using content as the basic element, we can design a solution at the content-level and achieve the intended purpose of that content efficiently. We can also identify the data packets that belong to a certain type of service, so that devices in the network can execute certain rules based on the service requirement, thereby achieving the corresponding goals of that type of service efficiently.

From the perspective of application models, this book divides the communication modes in the network into one-to-one communication, one-to-many communication, and many-to-one communication, respectively. These three communication modes can cover the basic communication needs of today's Internet.

The three different communication modes are shown in Figs. 1.1, 1.2, and 1.3. When designing the corresponding solutions for addressing privacy and accountability issues under these communication modes, we need to consider different factors.

For example, in a one-to-one communication mode, we can consider using source address and destination address to identify user's behavior. This is a direct way to mark a user's communication behavior. However, in another communication mode, perhaps we need to consider content and other factors. For example, in a many-to-one communication mode, we can identify the user's behavior by marking the content requested by the user accurately. Because a set of source address and destination address is not important in this case, perhaps what we need to focus on is content. If we still use a set of source address and destination address to identify user's behavior, it will cause a lot of overhead. Because it needs multiple sets of address pairs to completely record the user's behavior. In a one-to-many communication mode, we can consider categorizing factors with the same characteristics, such as

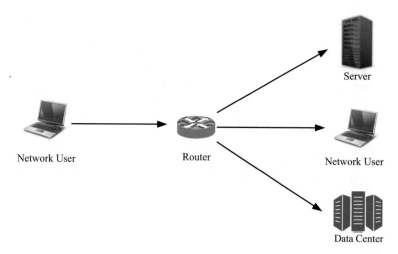

Fig. 1.2 The overview of the one-to-many communication mode

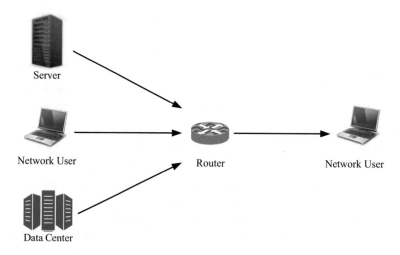

Fig. 1.3 The overview of the many-to-one communication mode

marking a user's one-time behavior or marking one type of behavior from the same user. We can then identify and record user's behavior based on this feature, rather than source or destination addresses or content. In this case, neither content nor addresses is what we need to focus on. For the many-to-many communication mode, we can choose one or more of the three basic communication modes as the basis, to meet the corresponding requirements according to the actual situation.

It should be noted that the types of entities in the three communication modes are not limited to users, servers, and data centers. In Figs. 1.1, 1.2 and 1.3 we only take these three entities as examples.

In this book, the schemes (i.e., architectures) introduced in Chaps. 4, 5 and 6 are content-based, flow-based, and service-based, respectively. Among them, the flow-based scheme corresponds to the one-to-one communication mode, the service-based scheme is based on the one-to-many communication mode, and the content-based scheme uses the many-to-one communication mode (from the perspective of a user requesting content). In addition, we choose Named Data Networking (NDN), a typical example of Information-Centric Networking (ICN) as a representative, to propose a scheme for future networks, because ICN has been considered as a promising development direction of future networks [27–29]. Therefore, the schemes introduced in this book can meet the needs of users in different application scenarios to protect their privacy, as well as the needs of managers to ensure that user behavior is accountable in the network.

1.6   Design Goals

We set several goals and evaluation indicators from three perspectives: basic functions, security and reliability, and performance improvement.

The basic functions include the following items:

- Protect user's identity, address and other private information.
- Identify malicious users in the network and hold them accountable when necessary.
- Achieve a balance between privacy protection and behavior accountability.

These three basic functions correspond to privacy protection, behavior accountability and balancing privacy and accountability, respectively.

The security and reliability include the following items:

- Prevent third parties from knowing what content is transmitted between users.
- Reduce the risk of leaking privacy by third parties.
- Improve the reliability of third parties (even if some nodes are down).
- Allow users to choose service providers who provide privacy protection and behavior accountability services.
- Detect malicious behaviors and identify malicious users in time (as fast as possible).
- Identifiers should be self-certifying.
- Should have strong scalability.

The performance improvement is mainly from the following aspects:

- The information used for verification may not be completely dependent on the packet.
- Reduce bandwidth overhead.
- Reduce the delay (e.g., reducing the delay in obtaining verification results).

In summary, the basic goal of the schemes introduced in this book (see Chaps. 4, 5, 6 and 7) are to protect the privacy of users, and at the same time to locate malicious users when malicious behaviors occur in the network. After locating malicious users, we can then prevent their malicious behaviors. In these schemes, third parties are required to help users hide privacy information such as their addresses.

Although in the schemes introduced in this book, the third party will not know the specific content transmitted by sender and receiver, a single third party still has a high risk of being attacked. Therefore, the schemes proposed in this book will effectively reduce the risk of leaking privacy by reducing the power of third parties, and improve the ability of third parties to provide services in a stable manner.

To achieve privacy protection and behavior accountability, the schemes introduced in this book mainly include three processes: sending information for identity verification, verifying the user's identity, and stopping malicious transmissions. These three processes have different implementation methods in different schemes, and the information or content delivered are also different. We will introduce them in detail in the subsequent chapters.

To make the information used for verification in our schemes independent of packets, we propose a series of self-certifying identifiers. The corresponding schemes can be implemented based on content, flow, and service. In the evaluation, we mainly evaluate the cost and delay in implementing these schemes. If the delay of information transmission during the verification process is reduced, it means that the scheme's ability to deal with malicious behaviors is improved, which will help network managers to discover malicious behaviors in the network in time.

1.7 Organization of the Proposed Book

The organization of this book is shown in Fig. 1.4. We introduce recent related work in Chap. 3 to explain why encryption technology is not enough to protect user privacy. Chapters 4, 5, 6 and 7 introduce the schemes we proposed for different levels (e.g., content, flow, and service) and different application scenarios based on the basic design principles (see Sect. 2.3). The main content of each chapter is presented below.

In this chapter, we introduce the research background of the proposed book, explain the research significance of this book and the problems that need to be solved. We introduce the views on privacy and accountability from different perspectives, i.e., from the perspective of users and managers. In addition to these, we divide the communication mode into three basic modes. The schemes introduced in the proposed book will cover these three basic communication modes.

In Chap. 2, we introduce the studies related to this book. In addition to introducing the research in the areas of privacy protection and behavior accountability, this chapter also introduces new network architectures and emerging network technologies.

In Chap. 3, we introduce a method based on machine learning that can be used to identify encrypted traffic. The results show that this method has a high recognition rate. The purpose of this chapter is to show that encryption is not enough to protect user privacy, which may be different from what people naturally think.

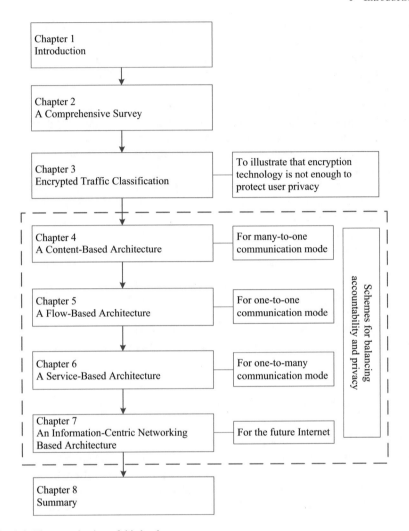

Fig. 1.4 The organization of this book

In Chap. 4, we introduce a content-based scheme to balance privacy protection and behavior accountability. In this chapter, we introduce the detailed design of the scheme, the design concept and generation method of the content identifier. We discuss possible problems with the deployment of the scheme and the corresponding solutions, and describe how to evaluate the performance and overhead of the scheme in detail. Readers can refer to our evaluation methods in their similar works.

In Chap. 5, we introduce a scheme for balancing privacy protection and behavior accountability based on network flows, and in Chap. 6 we introduce a service-based scheme that has the same purpose but uses a different approach. In Chap. 7, we introduce a scheme to achieve a balanced privacy and accountability in the ICN. The organization of these chapters is similar to Chap. 4.

In Chap. 8, we summarize this book and introduce directions for further research.

1.8 Summary

Privacy protection and behavior accountability are both necessary factors that are conducive to promoting the development of the Internet. Therefore, it is necessary to systematically and comprehensively study these two factors. There is an urgent need to innovate in technology, so that technical support can be provided to balance privacy and accountability, rather than only through legal and ethical aspects.

References

1. Clark DD, Wroclawski J, Sollins KR, Braden R (2005) Tussle in cyberspace: defining tomorrow's internet. IEEE/ACM Trans Netw 13(3):462–475
2. Ghaderi J, Srikant R (2010) Towards a theory of anonymous networking. In: IEEE conference on computer communications (INFOCOM). IEEE, pp 649–686
3. Wang N, Fu J, Zeng J, Bhargava BK (2018) Source-location privacy full protection in wireless sensor networks. Inf Sci 444:105–121
4. Isdal T, Piatek M, Krishnamurthy A, Anderson, T (2010) Privacy-preserving P2P data sharing with OneSwarm. In: Proceedings of the ACM SIGCOMM conference (SIGCOMM). ACM, pp 111–122
5. Ma X, Yang LT, Xiang Y, Zeng WK, Zou D, Jin H (2017) Fully reversible privacy region protection for cloud video surveillance. IEEE Trans Cloud Comput 5(3):510–522
6. Zhang G, Yang Y, Chen J (2012) A historical probability based noise generation strategy for privacy protection in cloud computing. J Comput Syst Sci 78(5):1374–1381
7. Ren J, Wu J (2010) Survey on anonymous communications in computer networks. Comput Commun 33(4):420–431
8. Raghavan B, Kohno T, Snoeren AC, Wetherall D (2009) Enlisting ISPs to improve online privacy: IP address mixing by default. In: International symposium on privacy enhancing technologies symposium. Springer, pp 143–163
9. Dingledine R, Mathewson N, Syverson P (2004) Tor: the second-generation onion router. In: Proceedings of the USENIX security symposium. USENIX
10. Bender A, Spring N, Levin D, Bhattacharjee B (2007) Accountability as a service. In: Proceedings of the USENIX workshop on steps to reducing unwanted traffic on the internet. USENIX, pp 5:1–5:6
11. Ilyas MU, Shafiq MZ, Liu AX, Radha H (2013) Who are you talking to? Breaching privacy in encrypted IM networks. In: IEEE international conference on network protocols (ICNP). IEEE, pp 1–10
12. Sung M, Xu J, Li J, Li L (2008) Large-scale IP traceback in high-speed internet: practical techniques and information-theoretic foundation. IEEE/ACM Trans Netw 16(6):1253–1266
13. Küsters R, Truderung T, Vogt A (2010) Accountability: definition and relationship to verifiability. In: Proceedings of the ACM conference on computer and communications security (CCS). ACM, pp 526–535
14. Liu J, Xiao Y (2011) Temporal accountability and anonymity in medical sensor networks. Mobile Netw Appl 16(6):695–712

15. Ko RK, Jagadpramana P, Mowbray M, Pearson S, Kirchberg M, Liang Q, Lee BS (2011) TrustCloud: a framework for accountability and trust in cloud computing. In: IEEE world congress on services. IEEE, pp 584–588
16. Xiao Z, Kathiresshan N, Xiao Y (2016) A survey of accountability in computer networks and distributed systems. Sec Commun Netw 9(4):290–315
17. Xiao Y (2009) Flow-net methodology for accountability in wireless networks. IEEE Netw 23(5):30–37
18. Madden M, Rainie L (2015) Americans' attitudes about privacy, security and surveillance. Pew Research Center
19. Olmstead K, Smith A (2017) Americans and cybersecurity. Pew Research Center
20. Bartlett J (2015) The dark net: inside the digital underworld. Melville House
21. Nunes E, Diab A, Gunn A, Marin E, Mishra V, Paliath V, Robertson J, Shakarian J, Thart A, Shakarian P (2016) Darknet and deepnet mining for proactive cybersecurity threat intelligence. In: IEEE conference on intelligence and security informatics (ISI). IEEE, pp 7–12
22. Cisco: Cisco visual networking index: forecast and trends, 2017–2022 white paper (2019)
23. Wu Y, Hu F, Min G, Zomaya AY (2017) Big data and computational intelligence in networking. CRC Press
24. Fred SB, Bonald T, Proutiere A, Régnié G, Roberts JW (2001) Statistical bandwidth sharing: a study of congestion at flow level. In: Proceedings of the conference on applications, technologies, architectures, and protocols for computer communications (SIGCOMM). ACM, pp 111–122
25. Dai HN, Wong RCW, Wang H (2017) On capacity and delay of multichannel wireless networks with infrastructure support. IEEE Trans Vehi Technol 66(2):1589–1604
26. Huang C, Min G, Wu Y, Ying Y, Pei K, Xiang Z (2017) Time series anomaly detection for trustworthy services in cloud computing systems. IEEE Trans Big Data
27. Xylomenos G, Ververidis CN, Siris VA, Fotiou N, Tsilopoulos C, Vasilakos X, Katsaros KV, Polyzos GC (2013) A survey of information-centric networking research. IEEE Commun Sur Tutor 16(2):1024–1049
28. Ahlgren B, Dannewitz C, Imbrenda C, Kutscher D, Ohlman B (2012) A survey of information-centric networking. IEEE Commun Mag 50(7):26–36
29. Zhang L, Afanasyev A, Burke J, Jacobson V, Crowley P, Papadopoulos C, Wang L, Zhang B et al (2014) Named data networking. ACM SIGCOMM Comput Commun Rev 44(3):66–73

Chapter 2
A Comprehensive Survey

This chapter provides details of the existing work related to our study. It introduces the schemes related to privacy protection and behavior accountability in Sect. 2.1. In this book, we not only provide the solutions designed for existing network architectures, but also propose innovative mechanisms for future networks (see Chap. 7). Thus, Sect. 2.2 will briefly introduce Information-Centric Networking (ICN), which is a typical example of the well-known future network architectures. Section 2.3 will introduce several emerging network technologies and design concepts of new network architectures which have been used in the schemes (i.e., architectures) that will be introduced in this book. Then, the advantages of the solution implemented at the network layer rather than the application layer will be briefly analyzed in Sect. 2.4. Finally, Sect. 2.5 summarizes this chapter.

2.1 Privacy Protection and Behavior Accountability

This section will introduce the existing schemes for privacy protection[1] and behavior accountability.

2.1.1 Accountability and Privacy

How to achieve accountability and privacy in the network has been a challenging task and has received tremendous research efforts [1–6]. These efforts focus on either

---

[1]Privacy protection is also called privacy preserving.

© The Editor(s) (if applicable) and The Author(s), under exclusive license to Springer Nature Singapore Pte Ltd. 2020
Y. Ma et al., *Accountability and Privacy in Network Security*,
https://doi.org/10.1007/978-981-15-6575-5_2

Table 2.1 The comparison of different schemes

Scheme	Layer	Accountability	Privacy	Level
Tor [2]	Application layer	No	Yes	Session
LAP [4]	Network layer	No	Yes	Session
AIP [1]	Network layer	Yes	No	Packet
APIP [7]	Network layer	Yes	Yes	Packet
Chapter 4 [8]	Network layer	Yes	Yes	Content
Chapter 5 [9]	Network layer	Yes	Yes	Flow
Chapter 6 [10]	Network layer	Yes	Yes	Service

accountability or privacy. Only a few studies have attempted to strike a balance between privacy and accountability [7].

Table 2.1 summarizes the differences between several well-known schemes and makes a comparison with the proposed architectures in this book (more details on the architectures proposed in this book will be discussed in Chaps. 4, 5 and 6).

Among the schemes listed in Table 2.1, Tor is an application layer tool that can be used to protect user privacy. Lightweight Anonymity and Privacy (LAP), Accountable Internet Protocol (AIP), and Accountable and Private Internet Protocol (APIP) work at the network layer. In these studies, LAP focuses on privacy protection, and AIP is designed for accountability. Although APIP is proposed to balance privacy and accountability, its implementation requires operations on all data packets, and the third party may disclose the user's information. To address the shortcomings of the existing studies, we have designed multiple schemes and will introduce them in this book [8–12]. These schemes address privacy and accountability issues at multiple levels, including content-level, flow-level, and service-level.

2.1.2 Behavior Accountability

The "behavior accountability" in the Internet plays an important role in maintaining a good degree of security of the network. The key to achieving accountability is to ensure the traceability and auditability of network behaviors, which requires an accurate grasp of the identity of users in the network [13, 14]. Therefore, the network should strengthen the certification of the source of the packet.

AIP [1] was the most famous solution whose primary objective is accountability. In the AIP architecture, the network is composed of accountability domains (ADs). Each accountability domain contains a series of nodes such as hosts and routers. The design of the AD facilitates the management of the network, as various management measures can be implemented in the units of ADs. In AIP, each host maintains a small cache to store the hash of recently sent packets. The first-hop router verifies the packet by challenging the source with the hash of a packet it sent. If not successfully verified, the packet is dropped by the router, and a verification packet is sent to the source. When a packet traverses the boundary of an AD, the previous AD where the packets originate must determine whether the source address is valid. In AIP, a victim host can send an explicit shutoff instruction to the host that generates such traffic to stop an attack. In addition to the AIP architecture, there are some studies that provide solutions for accountability IP addresses [15–20].

Besides enhancing the credibility and auditability of the source (e.g., IP addresses) of packets, there are studies that use reputation management techniques to manage and constrain user behavior [21]. In a reputation management mechanism, each participant is given a reputation value that is continually updated based on the reliability of the content provided by the participant, i.e., the reputation value is dynamically adjusted based on the participant's behavior. For users whose reputation value is declining, network managers can take steps to limit their behaviors and even punish them [21, 22]. Several studies achieve accountability through logging mechanisms [13, 14].

2.1.3 Privacy Protection

In addition to the related work considering accountability only, some existing solutions addressed privacy protection only. For instance, Tor [2] is one of the most popular projects for protecting user privacy. In its onion routing, instead of making socket connections directly to a responding machine, Tor makes connections through a sequence of machines called onion routers. Onion routing allows anonymous connections for both the requester and the sender. The Tor protocol (or Tor network) can effectively protect user privacy. The main drawback is obvious in that we might never determine who is responsible for illegal behavior.

Furthermore, LAP [4] is another work designed to privacy protection. It attempts to enhance anonymity by obscuring the topological location of an end-user based on two building blocks: packet-carried forwarding state and forwarding-state encryption. LAP allows each packet to carry its own forwarding state, and thus, the accountability domain can determine the next hop from the packet instead of retaining the per-flow state locally. In each AD, a private key was used to encrypt/decrypt forwarding information in the packet header, preventing other ADs from obtaining the packet forwarding information.

Some IPv6-based communications, as envisioned in the Internet-of-Things (IoT) scenarios, allow an individual host to be multi-addressed or to change addresses over time for privacy protection [5].

2.1.4 *Balancing Privacy and Accountability*

Privacy and accountability are two critical factors to ensure cybersecurity, and neither is dispensable. However, efforts were seldom made to consider the effects of both accountability and privacy, until when APIP [7] was proposed to solve the balancing problem between these two factors in packet-based networks under a one-to-one communication mode.

In APIP, a delegate was proposed to act as a third party to help hide the sender identity and vouch for the senders. The sender issued a packet with the accountability address instead of the source address as the return address. At the same time, a message will be forwarded to the accountability delegate to notify what had been issued by the sender. The message sent to the accountability delegate contains the user's ID and the fingerprint of the packet. A fingerprint is composed of a symmetric key, the packet header, and the hash of the packet. The receiver of the packets and routers along the packet transmission path can verify the received packets by sending a verification message to challenge the accountability delegate. The verification message includes the hash of the packet to be validated and the header of the packet. When the received packet is found to be malicious or illegal, the receiver or routers can send instructions to the delegate to stop the delegate from verifying the data. In APIP, the feasibility of delegate accountability had technically been proved.

Since APIP is implemented based on data packets, it requires a large amount of computing resources and storage resources, which may affect network performance. That is because the fingerprint in APIP architecture contains information about the packet header, and, thus can be only used for verifying the packets in a given flow.

In addition, APIP lacks measures to restrict third parties, and delegates are at risk, so the security and reliability of APIP in use also need to be improved. In APIP, if the instruction (issued to delegate) of stopping verification is used, the communicating parties will not be able to continue communication, which will affect the normal network participants. Because the two parties may not be malicious users, only some of their identifiers are used by malicious users, which affects their normal communication. At the same time, if the accountability delegate used to provide verification service is located in the source domain only, the access burden to this delegate will go up along with the increase in network traffic. It is intolerable for the delay-sensitive applications if the verification needs to be performed by the accountability delegate located far away from the verifier.

There are also some studies that combine encryption technology with reputation management technology to protect the confidentiality of user data, and to manage and constrain the behavior of users by assessing the credibility of users. As mentioned above, if only the encryption technology is used to encrypt the content sent by the user, it is impossible to ensure that the behavior of users (i.e., sending the data packet) is protected. Therefore, some studies have proposed reputation management mechanisms with certain anonymity [23].

Such mechanisms provide anonymous methods to protect the privacy of participants and update the reputation value through an additional redemption process after the data has been transmitted. However, in such schemes, malicious users in the network can deliberately maintain a high reputation value for a period of time, and then play a malicious role at critical moments, thereby affecting the effectiveness of the scheme in actual use [22].

In this book, we need to consider the advantages and shortcomings of existing solutions, and propose a series of mechanisms and designs that can achieve privacy protection and behavior accountability in the network.

2.2 Privacy and Accountability in Information-Centric Networking

Information-Centric Networking (ICN) is a promising future network architecture in which the content rather than its location becomes the core of the communication model [24, 25]. The birth of ICN is also due to the changes in the needs of users in the network, i.e., content transmission has become the main application requirement in the network.

As a typical ICN, the Named Data Networking (NDN) [26, 27] has received increasing attentions in recent years [12, 28–30]. NDN is a content-centric, name-based new Internet architecture. In NDN, users can obtain contents from nearby nodes, rather than requesting contents from distant producers or data centers. Therefore, NDN can greatly improve the efficiency of content delivery.

2.2.1 An Overview of Named Data Networking

In NDN, the one requesting the content is called the *consumer*, and the original source of the content (i.e., the one that produced the content) is called the *producer*. There are two types of packets in the NDN architecture, i.e., Interest packet and Data packet.

When a consumer wants to get a content, it will send an Interest packet to the surrounding nodes. When a node receives the Interest packet, it will query whether it has the cache of the content. If it has cached the content, the Data packet will carry the corresponding content (cached in the node) back to the consumer. If the node does not cache this content, it will forward the Interest packet to other nodes. The Interest packet will continue being forwarded until there is a node that can respond to the request. If a content is new, or there is no cache of the content in the network, the Interest packet will eventually be forwarded to the producer of the content. Figure 2.1 shows the forwarding process in the NDN architecture. The Pending Interest Table (PIT) records all the Interest packets that have been forwarded but the content has not been returned. For each Interest packet, the node decides when and where to forward the Interest packet according to the forwarding strategy [31–33].

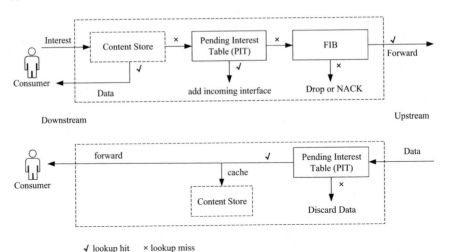

Fig. 2.1 An overview of the NDN architecture [27]

Although the NDN architecture is designed by taking security into consideration, there are still potential security issues. For example, consumer's privacy information (e.g., what content the consumer requests) may be obtained by other nodes, and the NDN architecture lacks effective way of accountability to consumer's behavior [34]. In the following, we will introduce the potential risks in NDN from the perspective of privacy disclosure and behavior accountability.

2.2.2   Privacy Disclosure Risks in NDN

In the NDN architecture, both the name and cache of a content may reveal the network user's privacy. The problem of name privacy in NDN is that the "Name" contains too much information; especially, the definition of names in human-readable formats poses a great challenge to the network in protecting the privacy of users [35]. An attacker can easily obtain the user's behavior from the name carried by the Interest packet or the Data packet. Content privacy is another problem in the NDN architecture. In addition to the risks of name privacy, the cache that exists in the NDN architecture may also reveal the user's privacy. In-network caching is a fundamental part of the NDN architecture, which helps reduce the delay in content retrieval and the bandwidth consumption in content transmission. However, an attacker can therefore infer whether the surrounding nodes have obtained some particular content by requesting specific content and recording the time to obtain the content, and even link the behavior to the particular consumers [36].

2.2.3   Lack of Accountability in NDN

In terms of behavior accountability, in NDN, a content will be signed by its producer [37]. Therefore, network managers (e.g., governments or ISPs) as well as consumers can thus find the producers who generate malicious content, and then punish them. This design enables the NDN architecture to have the ability to restrict content producers. If a content is harmful or illegal, consumers can find the producer of the content through the signature carried in the Data packet. However, the NDN architecture does not require consumers to sign the Interest packet, resulting in the situation that the accountability of consumers cannot be performed [34]. Although this design helps protect the privacy of consumers, it prevents network managers from finding malicious consumers. If a consumer attempts to interfere with the network by sending malicious requests (e.g., a malicious consumer sends a large number of Interest packets), how will the NDN architecture determine which consumer needs to be punished? How to stop an attack in time and how to effectively trace and find malicious consumers after an attack to determine which consumer needs to be punished have become challenging issues in NDN architecture.

Considering that in NDN, the protection of consumer privacy needs to be further strengthened, and the ability to monitor consumer behavior also needs to be improved. Therefore, in this book, we will propose a new scheme that can be used to balance privacy and accountability in the NDN architecture in Chap. 7.

2.3   Design Concepts Used in the Proposed Book

Many new network architectures, including NDN, XIA, MobilityFirst, NEBULA, etc. [27, 38–40], have considered the problems and possible solutions in the current network. If we can refine the concept of these new network architectures in the security design, and then combine the emerging network technologies, we could solve a series of security issues in the current network, including privacy and accountability. For example, through summarization and analysis, we find that the future network architecture has the characteristics of network sub-regional autonomy, self-certifying of identifiers, and decentralized design. This section will introduce these design concepts and new technologies which will be widely used in the solutions presented in this book.

2.3.1   Network Domain

In the design of future network architectures, the concept that the network is divided into domains for management has appeared many times. Similar designs exist in the

current network architecture, such as different local area networks (LANs) intercon-
nected to form a larger network.

In the mechanisms proposed in this book, we also divide the network into different
domains. For example, we refer to different network management scopes such as the
sender's network domain and the recipient's network domain. By dividing different
autonomous networks, we can achieve independent deployment, operation, and management of each network domain. The network domain can be divided according to
the requirements of departments, regions, applications, etc., which will enable the
network to have the ability of responding to rapid changes in demand and make network management more convenient. The isolation of different network domains can
block viruses from other domains, avoid large-scale attacks, and effectively control
risks.

2.3.2 Self-certifying Identifier

In recent years, many research efforts have been made on new types of network
addresses, most of which emphasize self-certifying [41]. Self-certifying means that
an entity (e.g., sender) claims to have an identity, and other entities can verify whether
the identity belongs to the claimant without third-party participation. If a node disguises the sender, it can be discovered by the following steps:

1. The verifier sends a random nonce N to the one that declares itself to be the sender.
   It should be noted that the generation of random numbers is out of the scope of
   this book.
2. The sender encrypts the random nonce N using its private key, and then sends the
   encrypted N to the verifier.
3. The verifier decrypts the encrypted random number N using the public key and
   determines whether the random number N is what it was sent to the sender.

The self-certifying identifiers have been widely adopted in a variety of distributed
systems. For example, in [42], self-certifying was established by binding three different entities: Real-World Identity (RWI), name, and public key. To achieve the
goal of self-certifying name in the AIP [1], the name of an object is considered as
the public key or the hash of the public key that corresponds to that object. In the
NSF-funded MobilityFirst project [38], a self-certifying Globally Unique Identifier
(GUID) was derived simply as a one-way hash of the public key, which was then used
to support the authentication and security throughout the project. In Host Identity
Protocol (HIP) [43], which was standardised by IETF, the host identifier was also
derived by a fixed-size hash of the public key.

The use of self-certifying identifiers can be considered as a trend in future networks [38, 41, 42]. In the architectures described in this book, the self-certifying
of identifiers is an important design concept and has been applied to the design of
each architecture. In this book, we identify and define entities and communication

behaviors in the communication process based on the actual needs. The character-istics of different application scenarios are considered in the design of identifiers. Therefore, the proposed identifier can efficiently identify entities and behaviors, and has uniqueness and self-certifying characteristics, which can reduce the complexity and overhead of the network. In addition, self-certifying identifiers help to establish trusted mechanisms in the network.

In addition to self-certifying capabilities, when designing identifiers that can iden-tify users, we should also consider the concept of separation of identifiers and loca-tions. In the current network architecture, the IP address not only represents the identity of a user, but also shows the user's location. Separating the user's identifier from the user's location is also considered to be the development trend of the future network [38, 39, 44].

2.3.3 Use of Independent Third Parties

The existence of third parties usually plays a balanced role. In real life, there are some tasks that require the intervention of a third party to be successfully completed. For example, when a customer uses a shopping website (e.g., Taobao, a very popular shopping website in China) to purchase goods or services, Alipay acts as a third party, deducting the corresponding amount of money from customers' account. When the customer receives the purchased goods, Alipay will transfer the money to the merchant's account. If the customer does not receive the purchased goods, or the transaction is in dispute, the relevant department of Taobao will intervene to deal with it. If the official of Taobao website determines that the merchant has violated the rules, the transaction will be cancelled and the temporarily deducted money will be returned to the customer's account. Without Alipay as a third party, customers may need to transfer money directly to the merchant's account when purchasing goods. Once the transaction is disputed, the settlement process will be more complicated. There is another common example. In the auction, the organization that organizes the auction also plays the role of a third party.

This shows that a third party can be used to balance the rights and obligations of both parties (e.g., sender and receiver). A third party can place the two parties who are associated in a relatively fair environment.

In this book, "Delegate" is designed as an independent third party. The delegate can be deployed on a server, router, or other specialized devices in the network to help hide the user's identity information and restrict the user's behavior. The delegate has three basic responsibilities in the proposed book: (1) protecting the privacy of their clients, (2) verifying packets via fingerprints or cached verification information, and realizing the accountability to their clients, and (3) dropping (stopping verifying) invalid or malicious packets if needed.

In the schemes proposed in this book, delegates will not know the specific content sent or received by users, and the content transmitted between users will be effectively protected. At the same time, a delegate is not responsible for the validity and security of the content, but acts as an independent third party to provide the guarantee for the user's true identity, which can confirm that the user exists.

When a user has malicious behavior and is reported, the delegate will take some measures to prevent the malicious behavior from continuing. Subsequent chapters in this book (see Chaps. 4, 5, 6 and 7) will explain when and under what conditions the delegate will take actions to prevent the spread of malicious behaviors in time.

What is harmful if a delegate is no longer trusted? Client privacy may be released, and the verification function may not be performed, or the incorrect verification results may be sent. Thus, the delegate cannot take the role of accountability, and the clients can decide to replace the delegate and take legal measures to punish the delegates [7, 45].

In addition to deploying multiple delegates in a network domain for users to choose from, to improve the security and reliability of the proposed schemes, we have designed a "Registry" to reduce the function of delegates and reduce the risk of user privacy leakage which might be caused by the delegate being attacked or even controlled. The Registry proposed in this book is responsible for generating, distributing, and managing the client's real identity. In addition, we use Client ID (see Chaps. 4 and 5) or User ID (see Chaps. 6 and 7) to represent users in this book. These two IDs can be regarded as the users' aliases, which are different from unique and unchangeable identity identifiers, and can be replaced as needed. It should be noted that the role of Client ID and User ID is the same. For the sake of convenience of description, we use different names in different chapters. We can also use other names to refer to aliases of network users. A Client ID can be generated by the hash of the sender's public key and a random number (i.e., nonce): Client ID $= H(K^+_{sender} \| nonce)$.

The relationships between the Client (e.g., senders), the Delegate, and the Registry are shown in Fig. 2.2, and their interactions can be described as follows:

1. A client registers a Client ID with the registry. Only the registry knows the mapping between the Client ID and the client's identity. Since the registry does not participate in the process of requesting or sending content by the client, the reg-

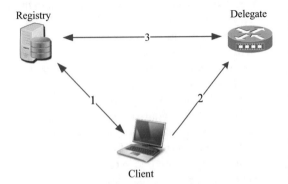

Fig. 2.2 The relationships between client, delegate, and registry

Registry

Delegate

3

1

2

Client

istry will not know the specific behavior of the client in the network (such as what content is requested or what content is sent).

2. A client sends the information for verification to the delegate.
3. When a content is judged to be malicious, or a client is judged to be a malicious user, the delegate needs to cooperate with the registry to check the user's true information and hold the user accountable for his/her actions. It should be noted that before cooperating with the registry to obtain the user's real identity, the delegate can still complete continuous measures to prevent malicious behavior.

Thus, delegates do not learn the real identity of a client, because the Client ID is only the flexible and replaceable alias of a client. If the delegate is attacked or even controlled, it will not reveal the user's real identity information. That is because the user can often use a new Client ID to replace the identifier in the packet header of the message sent to the delegate. Therefore, the design of the registry decentralizes the delegate's rights, and this decentralized design helps improve the security and reliability of the proposed architectures [46, 47].

2.3.4 Decentralization of Networks and Systems

In the future network architecture, we can observe that the decentralized design has been widely used. In addition to the network domain management that reflects the decentralized design concept, in the ICN network architectures (such as NDN), the content requested by the user comes from various places, which enables users to efficiently obtain content, and also effectively reduce or even avoid the risk of network service interruption caused by partial node failure. That is because, even if some nodes in the network cannot provide services, users can get content or services from other nodes in time.

In addition, since Bitcoin first proposed in 2008, blockchain technology has received increasing attention from academia and industry [48]. Decentralization is the core concept of blockchain technologies and a key factor for its widespread adoption. The blockchain technology allows nodes to construct a chain of transaction information through a series of techniques such as digital signature, hash operation, and consensus mechanism without mutual trust, ensuring that the stored information cannot be tampered. Therefore, decentralized design can improve the security, stability and reliability of the network or system. In this book, the concept of decentralization is also applied.

2.4   Comparison of Mechanisms at the Network Layer and the Application Layer

The term "application layer" is used in the two models of computer networks, i.e., Internet Protocol Suite (TCP/IP) and Open Systems Interconnection Model (OSI Model). In TCP/IP Protocol Suite, the application layer contains communication protocols and interface methods for inter-process communication across computer networks [49]. According to ISO/IEC 7498-1, the application layer needs to provide OSI services that can be directly used by application-processes in the OSI model [50]. Observed from the actual effect, the function of the application layer is to enable users to access the network.

In the seven-layer OSI model, the network layer is located at the third layer, and it is the layer that provides data routing paths for network communications. Data is transmitted through the network path in the form of packets in an ordered format controlled by the network layer. In TCP/IP Protocol Suite, the Internet layer corresponds to the third layer of the OSI model, i.e., the network layer. In the TCP/IP model, the Internet layer is responsible for forwarding data packets in the network. The main function of the network layer (or Internet layer) is to send data from the source network to the destination network, which is also the process of routing [49].

The network layer and the application layer have different positions in the network and have different functions. When comparing different layers, there are many advantages to deploying security design or security protocols at the network layer [51, 52]. This is because the network layer forwards packets without dealing with the packet payload, and the intermediate routers can verify the content in terms of packets at any hop, helping the network operators detect the issues more efficiently. Therefore, the schemes proposed in this book have been designed at the network layer, and can be deployed in the network as protocols at the network layer.

2.5   Summary

This chapter provides details of the related work involved in this book. In the network, if we only protect the privacy of users, or only focus on accountability for user behaviors, it is not conducive to the development of the Internet. That is because this is unequal and unfair to the main participants and maintainers in the network. Existing studies have limitations. Therefore, we need to do further research on how to achieve a balance between privacy protection and behavior accountability.

In this chapter, we have also combined the design concepts of new network architectures and related emerging network technologies to illustrate the basic design in the research process of this book. We will introduce the proposed schemes in detail in later chapters. Readers will have a clearer understanding of how we can apply emerging network technologies to address problems in today's network architectures.

References

1. Andersen DG, Balakrishnan H, Feamster N, Koponen T, Moon D, Shenker S (2008) Accountable internet protocol (AIP). In: Proceedings of the ACM SIGCOMM conference (SIGCOMM). ACM, pp 339–350
2. Dingledine R, Mathewson N, Syverson P (2004) Tor: the second-generation onion router. In: Proceedings of the USENIX security symposium. USENIX
3. Hao F, Li S, Min G, Kim HC, Yau SS, Yang LT (2015) An efficient approach to generating location-sensitive recommendations in ad-hoc social network environments. IEEE Trans Serv Comput 8(3):520–533
4. Hsiao HC, Kim THJ, Perrig A, Yamada A, Nelson SC, Gruteser M, Meng W (2012) LAP: lightweight anonymity and privacy. In: IEEE symposium on security and privacy. IEEE, pp 506–520
5. Hummen R, Wirtz H, Ziegeldorf JH, Hiller J, Wehrle K (2013) Tailoring end-to-end IP security protocols to the internet of things. In: IEEE international conference on network protocols (ICNP). IEEE, pp 1–10
6. Li X, Wang Q, Dai HN, Wang H (2018) A novel friendly jamming scheme in industrial crowdsensing networks against eavesdropping attack. Sensors 18(6):1938
7. Naylor D, Mukerjee MK, Steenkiste P (2014) Balancing accountability and privacy in the network. In: Proceedings of the ACM SIGCOMM conference (SIGCOMM). ACM, pp 75–86
8. Ma Y, Wu Y, Li J, Ge J (2020) APCN: a scalable architecture for balancing accountability and privacy in large-scale content-based networks. Inf. Sci. 527:511–532
9. Ma Y, Wu Y, Ge J, Li J (2018) A flow-level architecture for balancing accountability and privacy. In: IEEE international conference on trust, security and privacy in computing and communications (TrustCom). IEEE, pp 984–989
10. Ma Y, Wu Y, Ge J, Li J (2017) A new architecture for anonymous use of services in distributed computing networks. In: IEEE international symposium on parallel and distributed processing with applications (ISPA). IEEE, pp 368–374
11. Ma Y, Wu Y, Ge J, Jun L (2018) An architecture for accountable anonymous access in the internet-of-things network. IEEE Access 6:14451–14461
12. Ma Y, Wu Y, Li J, Ge J (2018) A new architecture for distributed computing in named data networking. In: IEEE international conference on high performance computing and communications (HPCC). IEEE, pp 474–479
13. Xiao Y (2009) Flow-net methodology for accountability in wireless networks. IEEE Netw 23(5):30–37
14. Xiao Z, Kathiresshan N, Xiao Y (2016) A survey of accountability in computer networks and distributed systems. Secur Commun Netw 9(4):290–315
15. Liu X, Li A, Yang X, Wetherall D (2008) Passport: secure and adoptable source authentication. In: Proceedings of the USENIX symposium on networked systems design and implementation (NSDI). USENIX, pp 365–378
16. Bremler-Barr A, Levy H (2005) Spoofing prevention method. In: Proceedings IEEE annual joint conference of the IEEE computer and communications societies, vol 1. IEEE, pp 536–547
17. Snoeren AC, Partridge C, Sanchez LA, Jones CE, Tchakountio F, Kent ST, Strayer WT (2001) Hash-based IP traceback. In: Proceedings of the conference on applications, technologies, architectures, and protocols for computer communications (SIGCOMM). ACM, pp 3–14
18. Snoeren AC, Partridge C, Sanchez LA, Jones CE, Tchakountio F, Schwartz B, Kent ST, Strayer WT (2002) Single-packet IP traceback. IEEE/ACM Trans Netw 10(6):721–734
19. Shue CA, Gupta M, Davy MP (2008) Packet forwarding with source verification. Comput Netw 52(8):1567–1582
20. Wang H, Bose A, El-Gendy M, Shin KG (2005) IP easy-pass: a light-weight network-edge resource access control. IEEE/ACM Trans Netw 13(6):1247–1260

21. Kamvar SD, Schlosser MT, Garcia-Molina H (2003) The eigentrust algorithm for reputation management in P2P networks. In: Proceedings of the international conference on world wide web. ACM, pp 640–651
22. Ma L, Liu X, Pei Q, Xiang Y (2018) Privacy-preserving reputation management for edge computing enhanced mobile crowdsensing. IEEE Trans Serv Comput
23. Wang XO, Cheng W, Mohapatra P, Abdelzaher T (2013) Enabling reputation and trust in privacy-preserving mobile sensing. IEEE Trans Mob Comput 13(12):2777–2790
24. Ahlgren B, Dannewitz C, Imbrenda C, Kutscher D, Ohlman B (2012) A survey of information-centric networking. IEEE Commun Mag 50(7):26–36
25. Xylomenos G, Ververidis CN, Siris VA, Fotiou N, Tsilopoulos C, Vasilakos X, Katsaros KV, Polyzos GC (2013) A survey of information-centric networking research. IEEE Commun Surv Tutor 16(2):1024–1049
26. Jacobson V, Smetters DK, Thornton JD, Plass MF, Briggs NH, Braynard RL (2009) Networking named content. In: Proceedings of the international conference on emerging networking experiments and technologies (CoNEXT). ACM, pp 1–12
27. Zhang L, Afanasyev A, Burke J, Jacobson V, Crowley P, Papadopoulos C, Wang L, Zhang B et al (2014) Named data networking. ACM SIGCOMM Comput Commun Rev 44(3):66–73
28. Ge J, Wang S, Wu Y, Tang H, Yuepeng E (2016) Performance improvement for source mobility in named data networking based on global–local FIB updates. Peer-to-Peer Netw Appl 9(4):670–680
29. Ren Y, Li J, Shi S, Li L, Wang G, Zhang B (2016) Congestion control in named data networking—a survey. Comput Commun 86:1–11
30. Wu H, Li J, Zhi J (2015) MBP: a max-benefit probability-based caching strategy in information-centric networking. In: IEEE international conference on communications (ICC). IEEE, pp 5646–5651
31. Yuan H, Song T, Crowley P (2012) Scalable NDN forwarding: concepts, issues and principles. In: International conference on computer communications and networks (ICCCN). IEEE, pp 1–9
32. Dai H, Lu J, Wang Y, Pan T, Liu B (2016) BFAST: high-speed and memory-efficient approach for NDN forwarding engine. IEEE/ACM Trans Netw 25(2):1235–1248
33. Tariq A, Rehman RA, Kim BS (2019) Forwarding strategies in NDN based wireless networks: a survey. IEEE Commun Surve Tutor
34. Zhang X, Chang K, Xiong H, Wen Y, Shi G, Wang G (2011) Towards name-based trust and security for content-centric network. In: IEEE international conference on network protocols (ICNP). IEEE, pp 1–6
35. Tsudik G, Uzun E, Wood CA (2016) Ac3n: anonymous communication in content-centric networking. In: IEEE annual consumer communications & networking conference (CCNC). IEEE, pp 988–991
36. Acs G, Conti M, Gasti P, Ghali C, Tsudik G (2013) Cache privacy in named-data networking. In: IEEE international conference on distributed computing systems. IEEE, pp 41–51
37. Yu Y, Afanasyev A, Clark D, Jacobson V, Zhang L et al (2015) Schematizing trust in named data networking. In: Proceedings of the ACM conference on information-centric networking. ACM, pp 177–186
38. Venkataramani A, Kurose JF, Raychaudhuri D, Nagaraja K, Mao M, Banerjee S (2014) Mobilityfirst: a mobility-centric and trustworthy internet architecture. ACM SIGCOMM Comput Commun Rev 44(3):74–80
39. Han D, Anand A, Dogar F, Li B, Lim H, Machado M, Mukundan A, Wu W, Akella A, Andersen DG et al (2012) XIA: efficient support for evolvable internetworking. In: Proceedings of the USENIX symposium on networked systems design and implementation (NSDI). USENIX, pp 309–322
40. Anderson T, Birman K, Broberg R, Caesar M, Comer D, Cotton C, Freedman MJ, Haeberlen A, Ives ZG, Krishnamurthy A et al (2014) A brief overview of the NEBULA future internet architecture. ACM SIGCOMM Comput Commun Rev 44(3):81–86

41. Mazieres D, Kaminsky M, Kaashoek MF, Witchel E (1999) Separating key management from file system security. In: Proceedings of the ACM symposium on operating systems principles (SOSP). ACM, pp 124–139
42. Ghodsi A, Koponen T, Rajahalme J, Sarolahti P, Shenker S (2011) Naming in content-oriented architectures. In: Proceedings of the ACM SIGCOMM workshop on information-centric networking. ACM, pp 1–6
43. Nikander P, Moskowitz R (2006) Host identity protocol (HIP) architecture. RFC 4423
44. Ramírez W, Masip-Bruin X, Yannuzzi M, Serral-Gracia R, Martínez A, Siddiqui MS (2014) A survey and taxonomy of ID/locator split architectures. Comput Netw 60:13–33
45. Boukerche A, Ren Y (2008) A trust-based security system for ubiquitous and pervasive computing environments. Comput Commun 31(18):4343–4351
46. Ali M, Dhamotharan R, Khan E, Khan SU, Vasilakos AV, Li K, Zomaya AY (2017) SeDaSC: secure data sharing in clouds. IEEE Syst J 11(2):395–404
47. Lou W, Ren K (2009) Security, privacy, and accountability in wireless access networks. IEEE Wirel Commun 16(4):80–87
48. Underwood S (2016) Blockchain beyond bitcoin. Commun ACM 59(11):15–17
49. Forouzan BA (2002) TCP/IP protocol suite. McGraw-Hill, Inc
50. ISO (1994) Information technology–open systems interconnection–basic reference model: the basic model. ISO/IEC 7498-1: 1994(E)
51. Blaze M, Ioannidis J, Keromytis AD (1999) Trust management and network layer security protocols. In: International workshop on security protocols. Springer, pp 103–108
52. Luo H, Kong J, Zerfos P, Lu S, Zhang L (2004) URSA: ubiquitous and robust access control for mobile ad hoc networks. IEEE/ACM Trans Netw 12(6):1049–1063

Chapter 3
Encrypted Traffic Classification

With the increasing emphasis on information security by users, many encrypted traffic is being transmitted over the network. However, even if the data is encrypted, it is not enough to protect the privacy of users. There exist techniques to classify encrypted traffic. Although many studies on the classification of encrypted traffic claim that the purpose is for network management and/or anomaly detection. However, such techniques may be used to spy on the privacy of users.

This chapter introduces our recent study on encrypted traffic classification. It shows that traffic encryption is not enough to protect the user privacy. If the user's identity information cannot be protected, the user's behavior may still be revealed. Protecting users' identity information is the key for privacy protection. Combined with a variety of technologies including encryption technology, the users' privacy can be better protected.

3.1 Introduction

In recent years, traffic encryption has been widely used in the Internet. Traffic encryption technology can be used to protect the freedom, privacy and anonymity of Internet users, but it also allows users to evade detection by firewalls and circumvent surveillance systems. The abuse of encryption technology has brought new threats to network security and network management [2]. Therefore, the identification and classification of encrypted traffic has attracted significant attentions from both academia and industry.

Network traffic classification is a key technology of network management and can be used for traffic management, abnormal detection, and so on [3]. It has received tremendous efforts in researches and received remarkably satisfying results. How-

© The Editor(s) (if applicable) and The Author(s), under exclusive license
to Springer Nature Singapore Pte Ltd. 2020
Y. Ma et al., *Accountability and Privacy in Network Security*,
https://doi.org/10.1007/978-981-15-6575-5_3

ever, unlike the traditional classification of common network traffic, the rapid growth of encrypted network traffic poses additional challenges for traffic classification. The existing solutions to address traffic classification problems mainly fall into three main categories: port-based, payload-based (e.g., deep packet inspection), and machine learning based [4–6]. The classic port-based approach works well for the applications with a specific port number (e.g., FTP traffic with port 21). However, since many applications use dynamic ports, these methods are no longer reliable [7]. Deep packet inspection (DPI) can analyze the data of an entire packet and then identify the network protocols and applications to which the packet belongs. However, the use of DPI is almost impossible to properly analyze encrypted traffic. In addition, decrypting encrypted traffic is not feasible because it typically consumes a lot of computing resources. For machine learning methods used in traffic classification, excellent feature extraction methods and appropriate classification algorithms are required to achieve good performance.

When given network traffic, we first intend to figure out whether it is encrypted, and then identify which application category (e.g., P2P and VoIP) it belongs to. It is worth noting that if we can distinguish the application type of encrypted traffic, through combining the source address of the packet, we may speculate on the behavior of a user. In this way, the user's behavior information will be leaked. The difficulty in distinguishing which application the encrypted traffic belongs to is how to select the discriminant features for classification [8]. In most existing studies, features are designed and extracted by human experts [5, 6, 9]. This hand-crafted feature selection consumes much time and cannot find out the exact features generally.

There are only a few studies reported in the current literature that exploit the features automatically by using convolutional neural networks at the packet level [10, 11]. In these studies, using only one packet of a flow is not sufficient because other packets may contain different useful features (e.g., time sequence features between packets) for traffic classification. In this chapter, we present a new deep learning model for encrypted traffic classification [1]. In the proposed model, the effective convolutional neural network (CNN) is used for packet feature extraction, and the long short-term memory (LSTM) is used for timing feature extraction at the traffic level.

The rest of this chapter is constructed as follows: Sect. 3.2 elaborates the proposed model, including the data pre-processing and the architecture. Section 3.3 shows the experimental results based on the public dataset and the dataset collected from the backbone network of the China Science and Technology Network (CSTNET). Finally, Sect. 3.4 concludes this chapter.

3.2 The Proposed Model

Figure 3.1 illustrates the workflow of our encrypted traffic classification model. Before traffic is used as input, we need to split the traffic into discrete units. Generally, there are two kinds of granularity in traffic classification: packet-level and flow-level.

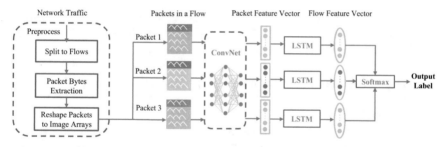

Fig. 3.1 The architecture of the proposed model

In this chapter, we follow the flow granularity, which is more common in both industry and academia. For each flow, we extract three consecutive packets. After the data pre-processing (Sect. 3.2.1), we generate the three packet images. Then, we feed the convolutional neural network (Sect. 3.2.2.1) with these three packet images. The outputs of the convolutional neural network are sent to the LSTM model (Sect. 3.2.2.2), which is followed by a softmax function and outputs the classification of this flow.

3.2.1 Data Pre-processing

The data pre-processing process consists of three steps, i.e., flow splitting, packet layer extraction, and reshaping packets to images. In what follows, we will introduce these steps separately.

3.2.1.1 Flow Splitting

In this chapter, the raw data traffic is split into flows according to the five tuples. For any flow f_i in the flow set: $F = \{f_1, f_2, f_3, \ldots\}$, the number of packets contained in f_i is n, i.e., $f_i = \{p_1^i, p_2^i, \ldots, p_n^i\}$, where p stands for a packet.

We select three consecutive packets at a random location in a flow f_i, which can be expressed as: $P = \{p_k^i, p_{k+1}^i, p_{k+2}^i\}$, where k is an integer in the range $[1, n-2]$. Formally, we will train a function f or a classifier that can identify the class to which the flow f_i belongs.

3.2.1.2 Packet Layer Extraction

In the proposed model, the packet bytes are used as the inputs of neural networks. Different packets have different lengths, however the input size of a neural network should be constant. Therefore, we need to limit the sampled packet bytes to a constant. In our approach, the length of the payload byte sequence of any packet in P equals to 784 bytes. First, we collect the header of a packet at the IP layer. In this chapter, we only consider the traffic with IPv4 addresses, so the header is 20 bytes. The TCP/UDP layer is involved in our packet payload sequence. We fill 12 zero bytes to the end of the UDP header (8 bytes) for alignment with the TCP header [11]. The remaining 744 bytes consist of the rest of the packet payload. If the payload length exceeds 744 bytes, we will truncate it. If the payload length is less than 744 bytes, it will be padded with zeros.

To avoid the case where the network learns the classification evidence only according to the five tuples instead of the unique patterns of each class, we anonymize the flow information by making them be zeros, aiming to improving the scalability of our model.

3.2.1.3 Reshaping Packets to Images

For any packet in P, we can obtain a 784-byte sequence. As we know, one byte can be transformed into an integer in the range of [0, 255]. Therefore, we can treat a byte as a pixel. For convenience in computing, the 784-byte sequence is reshaped into a 28×28 matrix. Correspondingly, the matrix can be constructed as an image with 28 pixel widths and 28 pixel heights. Finally, we normalize the scale to [0, 1] by dividing the byte by 255. In this way, we can generate three images that belong to a flow. The three images correspond to the three acquired packets in the flow. These three 28×28 images will be fed into the neural network for training and testing.

3.2.2 The Proposed Architecture

Deep learning has been successfully applied in many fields [12, 13]. In this chapter, we combine convolutional neural networks and recurrent neural networks in the proposed model.

Specifically, the convolutional neural network is used to mine features that are hidden inside a single packet image. It should be noted that these three packets share the same convolutional neural network, which has proven to be convenient and effective experimentally. The output of the convolutional neural network is represented as three packet feature vectors of the same dimension, which are fed into the recurrent neural network to extract the characteristics of a flow represented by the three packets. The recurrent neural network is implemented by using the flexible LSTM cells. At last, we set a softmax layer to the end of the output of LSTM for the ultimate classification results.

3.2.2.1 ConvNet for Packet Image Feature Extraction

As shown in Fig. 3.2, the convolutional neural network consists of two convolutional layers (i.e., Conv-1 and Conv-2) and a fully connect layer (Fc) in the proposed model. As for the design of the convolutional layer, we use the simple and effective VGG-net [14]. In Conv-1, a 28 × 28 image with 64 kernels is filtered twice, whose size is 3 × 3, corresponding to 3-grams bytes, with one stride. Relu [15] is employed as the activation function. After a 2 × 2 maxpooling layer, the output is sent to Conv-2, which has the same structure with Conv-1. Then, we take the output of Conv-2 to the dense layer with 256 units. To prevent over-fitting, the dropout layer with the 0.25 probability are added to the end of the Fc layer. We summarize the convolutional neural network part in Table 3.1. We can get a packet image feature vector with 256 dimensions for a packet. When training and testing, the convolutional part transfers the three 28 × 28 packet images into three 256-dimension packet feature vectors.

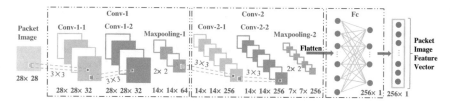

Fig. 3.2 The construct of the convolutional part in the proposed model

Table 3.1 The details of convolution

Layer	Name	Input	Filter	Stride	Output	Weight
Conv-1	Conv1-1	28 × 28	3 × 3 × 64	1	28 × 28 × 64	576
	Conv1–2	28 × 28 × 64	3 × 3 × 64	1	28 × 28 × 64	576
	Maxpooling-1	28 × 64	2 × 2	2	14 × 14 × 64	–
Conv-2	Conv1-1	14 × 14 × 64	3 × 3 × 128	1	14 × 14 × 128	1,152
	Conv1–2	14 × 14 × 128	3 × 3 × 128	1	14 × 14 × 128	1,152
	Maxpooling-2	14 × 14 × 64	2 × 2	2	7 × 7 × 128	–
Flat	Flatten	77,128	–	–	6,272	–
FC	Dense	6,272	–	–	256	1,605,632

3.2.2.2 LSTM for Flow Time Sequence Feature Extraction

In addition to the characteristics of a single packet, the time series features of a flow can also be useful in traffic classification. Recurrent neural networks have shown a considerable power for exploiting sequential tasks [16]. In this section, we implement the recurrent layer by using the LSTM cells. We forward the three 256-dimension packet feature vectors to the LSTM cells with the time sequence $T = 3$. The number of the hidden units in LSTM is set to 256. Furthermore, we set the output probability with 0.8 in the LSTM to avoid over-fitting problem. Finally, the outputs of the recurrent layer are fed into a c-way softmax function which produces a distribution over the c class labels. The variable c changes according to the number of the labeled classes in the dataset.

3.3 Performance Evaluation

In this section, we use the mechanism proposed in this chapter to classify VPN traffic and evaluate the effects of the proposed mechanism. Through evaluation, we also show the fact that machine learning technology can be used to identify encrypted traffic. This also means that it is not enough to protect the privacy of users only by encrypting the content transmitted by the user.

3.3.1 Datasets

In this section, two datasets are used for evaluation. The first one is the public ISCX VPN-nonVPN traffic dataset [17], published by the University of New Brunswick. For the convenience of description, in this section, we call it ISCX dataset, or the dataset coming from ISCX. The authors captured a regular session and a session over VPN, and the dataset has a total of 14 traffic categories, including VOIP, VPN-VOIP, P2P, VPN-P2P, etc. Before the evaluation, we re-mark the raw traffic for 12 classes according to the previous work [10].

The second dataset was collected from the actual network environment in the backbone network of the China Science and Technology Network (CSTNET). The size of the dataset collected from CSTNET is 175 GB, which was collected 16 times on different days and at different time. In this chapter, we use nDPI [18] to label the dataset collected from CSTNET. In this section, we call it CSTNET dataset, or the dataset coming from CSTNET.

The ISCX dataset is used to evaluate the effect of our model on VPN traffic, and the CSTNET dataset is used to evaluate the effect of our model on SSL traffic. In addition, the state-of-the-art study [10] (we call it 1D-CNN approach in this section) is compared with our model to show both efficiency and effectiveness.

Table 3.2 The labels in the dataset

Dataset	Type	Labels
ISCX	Non-VPN	Email, Chat, Streaming, File, VoIP, P2P
	VPN	VPN-Email, VPN-Chat, VPN-Streaming, VPN-File, VPN-VoIP, VPN-P2P
CSTNET	SSL	SSL.Amazon, SSL.Google, SSL.QQ, SSL.Apple, SSL.Microsoft, SSL.Sina, SSL.iQIYI

Table 3.2 provides the types and labels in the two datasets. The datasets are aggregated into lots of flows grouped by the five tuples (i.e., source IP, destination IP, source port, destination port, and protocol). We select three consecutive packets at a random location in a flow, and then randomly divide the dataset into a training part and a test part using the ratio of 8:2, respectively.

3.3.2 Evaluation Environment

In this evaluation, we employ a machine using Ubuntu 16.04 with 30 GB memory, and the GPU is the NVIDIA K80. As the same with most deep learning experiments, the one-hot encoding is applied to transforming the class labels for tensorflow. We set the penalty factor of L2 regularization as 0.05 [19]. The Adam [20] is used to update network weights iteratively with the initial learning rate at 1e-3 and a decay rate at 0.9 in every epoch. The mini-batch size is set to 64 and the learning procedure epochs are around 200.

3.3.3 Evaluation Metrics

To evaluate the performance of our model for traffic classification, we adopt the two common and widely-used metrics: precision and recall. These metrics are formulated as follows:

$$precision = \frac{TP}{TP + FP}$$
$$recall = \frac{TP}{TP + FN}$$

where TP and FP represent the number of items correctly and incorrectly labelled as belonging to the positive class, respectively. FN is the number of items incorrectly labelled as belonging to the negative class.

3.3.4 Evaluation Results and Analysis

Figures 3.3 and 3.4 show the performance on the ISCX dataset, i.e., the effect of our model on VPN traffic. Figures 3.5 and 3.6 depict the results when we use the CSTNET dataset, which reflect the effect of our model on SSL traffic.

Figures 3.3 and 3.4 show that the proposed model can effectively classify encrypted VPN traffic. It achieves the precision of 0.89 and recall of 0.89 on average, improving 3% if compared with the 1D-CNN approach [10].

As for the classification on the SSL traffic, Figs. 3.5 and 3.6 demonstrate that our model achieves the precision of 0.90 and recall of 0.89 on average on CSTNET dataset, improving 5% in precision and 3% in recall compared with the 1D-CNN approach [10].

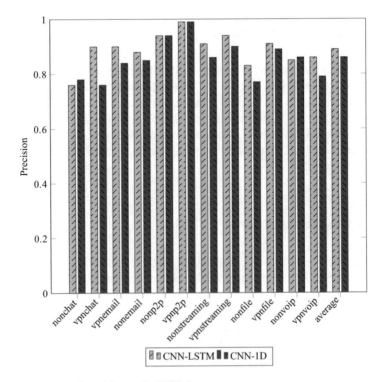

Fig. 3.3 The results of precision on the ISCX dataset

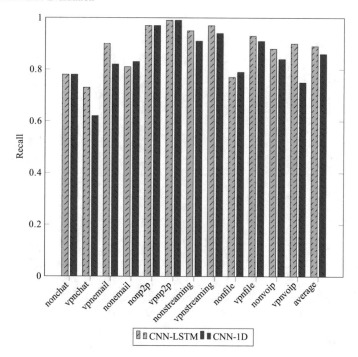

Fig. 3.4 The results of recall on the ISCX dataset

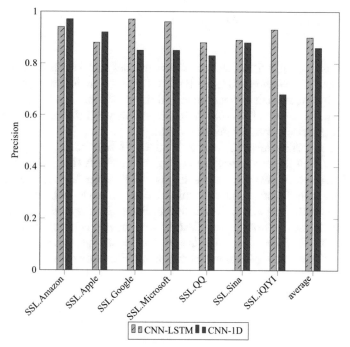

Fig. 3.5 The results of precision on the CSTNET dataset

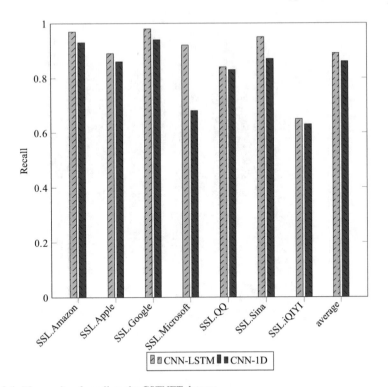

Fig. 3.6 The results of recall on the CSTNET dataset

From Figs. 3.3, 3.4, 3.5, 3.6, we can observe that our model has better performance and many advantages compared to the 1D-CNN approach in different types of traffic, indicating the effectiveness of our model. At the same time, it strongly proves that encrypted traffic cannot effectively protect the privacy of information such as user behavior (e.g., which websites the user visits).

For further detailed analysis, Figs. 3.7 and 3.8 illustrate the heatmap of the confused matrix with the row normalized on the two datasets (i.e., ISCX dataset and CSTNET dataset). As we can see, the diagonal line of the heatmap carries deeper orange color than the other squares, which means the model behaves the effective classification ability on the encrypted traffic. Figure 3.7 shows the lightest orange color points to the class of vpnfile. That is, our model is easy to classify the class of vpnfile into the class of nonvoip. One reason is that the number of the training samples on the class of vpnchat is less than that of the other classes. The other rea-

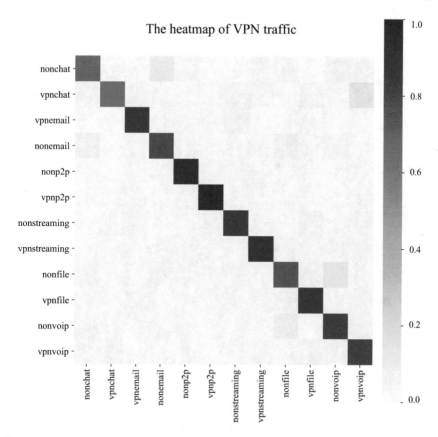

Fig. 3.7 The confusion matrix of the classification results with the row normalized on the ISCX dataset

son is that the captured traffic on the file transfer and voip are both collected on the Skype, which makes it difficult to classify for our model. In the evaluation, the proposed model only incorrectly classifies one of the non-VPN traffic classes into another non-VPN traffic classes, rather than VPN traffic classes. It therefore suggests we can almost identify the traffic when considering the only two classes of VPN and non-VPN traffic. Figure 3.8 shows the confused matrix of the classification result on the SSL traffic. The deep orange diagonal of the heatmap suggests that our model is able to classify the seven subtypes of SSL traffic. The lightest orange color corresponds to the class of SSL.iQiYi, which is a popular video website in China. That means our model behaves a little worse in classification of SSL.iQiYi than that of other subtypes, and we will amplify our datasets and improve our model in order to classify more types of SSL traffic effectively in the future.

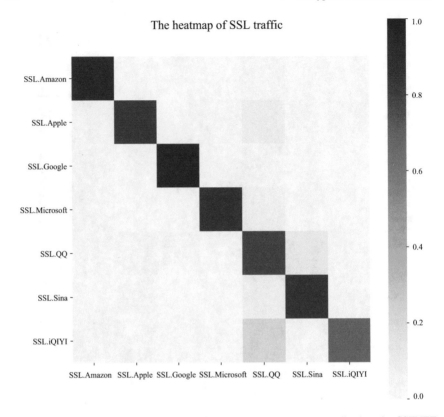

Fig. 3.8 The confusion matrix of the classification results with row normalized on the CSTNET dataset

3.4 Conclusions and Discussions

This chapter introduces a novel deep neural network that combines both the convolutional network and the recurrent network to classify encrypted traffic. The convolutional network has been used to extract the packet features for a single packet. The recurrent network has been trained to pick out the flow features based on the inputs of the packet features of any three consecutive packets in a flow. The proposed model has outperformed the existing studies which ask for the first N packets of a flow, and it has provided more flexibility in real practice. The evaluation results have shown that the machine learning method can effectively improve performance of encrypted traffic classification. It has further illustrated that only encrypting traffic is not sufficient to protect the privacy of users. This has also confirmed our view that it is necessary to propose new architectures that can protect the identity of users.

References

1. Zou Z, Ge J, Zheng H, Wu Y, Han C, Yao Z (2018) Encrypted traffic classification with a convolutional long short-term memory neural network. In: IEEE international conference on high performance computing and communications (HPCC). IEEE, pp 329–334
2. Dingledine R, Mathewson N, Syverson P (2004) Tor: the second-generation onion router. In: Proceedings of the USENIX security symposium. USENIX (2004)
3. Huang C, Min G, Wu Y, Ying Y, Pei K, Xiang Z (2017) Time series anomaly detection for trustworthy services in cloud computing systems. IEEE Transactions on Big Data
4. Yamansavascilar B, Guvensan MA, Yavuz AG, Karsligil ME (2017) Application identification via network traffic classification. In: International conference on computing, networking and communications (ICNC). IEEE, pp 843–848
5. Korczyński M, Duda A (2014) Markov chain fingerprinting to classify encrypted traffic. In: IEEE conference on computer communications (INFOCOM). IEEE, pp 781–789
6. Alshammari R, Zincir-Heywood AN (2011) Can encrypted traffic be identified without port numbers, IP addresses and payload inspection? Comput Netw 55(6):1326–1350
7. Zander S, Nguyen T, Armitage G (2005) Automated traffic classification and application identification using machine learning. In: The IEEE conference on local computer networks (LCN). IEEE, pp 250–257
8. Dainotti A, Pescape A, Claffy KC (2012) Issues and future directions in traffic classification. IEEE Netw 26(1):35–40
9. Sun GL, Xue Y, Dong Y, Wang D, Li C (2010) An novel hybrid method for effectively classifying encrypted traffic. In: IEEE global telecommunications conference (GLOBECOM). IEEE, pp 1–5
10. Wang W, Zhu M, Wang J, Zeng X, Yang Z (2017) End-to-end encrypted traffic classification with one-dimensional convolution neural networks. In: IEEE international conference on intelligence and security informatics (ISI). IEEE, pp 43–48
11. Lotfollahi M, Siavoshani MJ, Zade RSH, Saberian M (2017) Deep packet: a novel approach for encrypted traffic classification using deep learning. Soft Comput 1–14
12. Collobert R, Weston J (2008) A unified architecture for natural language processing: deep neural networks with multitask learning. In: Proceedings of the international conference on machine learning. ACM, pp 160–167
13. Krizhevsky A, Sutskever I, Hinton GE (2012) Imagenet classification with deep convolutional neural networks. In: Advances in neural information processing systems, pp 1097–1105
14. Simonyan K, Zisserman A (2014) Very deep convolutional networks for large-scale image recognition. arXiv preprint arXiv:1409.1556
15. Nair V, Hinton GE (2010) Rectified linear units improve restricted boltzmann machines. In: Proceedings of the international conference on machine learning, pp 807–814
16. Donahue J, Anne Hendricks L, Guadarrama S, Rohrbach M, Venugopalan S, Saenko K, Darrell T (2015) Long-term recurrent convolutional networks for visual recognition and description. In: Proceedings of the IEEE conference on computer vision and pattern recognition. IEEE, pp 2625–2634
17. Draper-Gil G, Lashkari AH, Mamun MSI, Ghorbani AA (2016) Characterization of encrypted and vpn traffic using time-related features. In: Proceedings of the international conference on information systems security and privacy, pp 407–414
18. Deri L, Martinelli M, Bujlow T, Cardigliano A (2014) nDPI: Open-source high-speed deep packet inspection. In: International wireless communications and mobile computing conference. IEEE, pp 617–622
19. Ng AY (2004) Feature selection, L1 vs. L2 regularization, and rotational invariance. In: Proceedings of the international conference on machine learning. ACM, p 78
20. Kingma DP, Ba J (2014) Adam: a method for stochastic optimization. arXiv preprint arXiv:1412.6980

Chapter 4
A Content-Based Architecture

This chapter introduces an architecture based on content that can be used to balance privacy protection and behavior accountability in the network. The terms *requester* and *receiver* are used interchangeably in this chapter, because the receiver acts as the content requester in content-based networks [1, 2]. In the network where content transmission is the main requirement, the content acquisition process is usually driven by requesters [3, 4]. Therefore, in this chapter, the proposed architecture is designed from the requester's point of view.

The remainder of this chapter is organized as follows. Section 4.1 briefly introduces the research background. The problem description is presented in Sect. 4.2. Section 4.3 describes the design of the proposed architecture. The details of the accountability process is shown in Sect. 4.4 and the theoretical analysis is presented in Sect. 4.5. The analysis of potential security issues in the real-world deployment of the proposed architecture is presented in Sect. 4.6. Section 4.7 conducts the performance results of the proposed content-based architecture. Finally, Sect. 4.8 concludes this chapter.

4.1 Introduction

Content access has become the dominant service in today's Internet. To support effective and scalable content distribution over the network, the current Internet is shifting towards a content-centric mode from a traditional host-oriented mode. The content-centric mode, e.g., peer-to-peer (P2P) networks and content delivery networks (CDNs), has been widely adopted by service providers (SPs) or content providers (CPs) for efficient file sharing and video transmission. The Cisco Visual Networking Index (VNI) recently predicted that CDNs will carry 72% of Internet

© The Editor(s) (if applicable) and The Author(s), under exclusive license
to Springer Nature Singapore Pte Ltd. 2020
Y. Ma et al., *Accountability and Privacy in Network Security*,
https://doi.org/10.1007/978-981-15-6575-5_4

traffic by 2022 up from 56% in 2017 [6]. This also reflects the growing demand for content transmission in the network.

The rapid growth of the Internet has given rise to new requirements and challenges in balancing accountability and privacy, especially in networks focused on content request and transmission. In the scenarios where the main purpose is to obtain content, the content requesters can come from more than one places. This type of communication belongs to many-to-one communication mode we described in Chap. 1. In this case, if we collect information for accountability based on each packet sent by the user, and if the same content sent to different users generates multiple messages for verification, it will require the network and devices (in the network) to provide more computing, storage, bandwidth and other resources. In addition, the characteristics of Internet traffic at the packet level are notoriously complex and extremely variable [7, 8]. Therefore, how to protect the privacy of Internet users, while monitoring their behaviors to perform accountability when necessary is important and a challenging task in large-scale content-based networks.

To fill in this research gap, we propose a new scalable architecture for balancing Accountability and Privacy in Content-based Networks (APCN) [5]. The APCN architecture was designed with respect to the unique characteristics of the content and content-based networks while accommodating the case of one-to-one communication mode. In APCN, we can perform appropriate operations at the "content" level. The design philosophy is to reduce the storage required for verification information and improve the network efficiency and scalability in large-scale content-based networks. In this chapter, we will introduce the proposed APCN architecture. In summary, the main contributions of this research are as follows:

- A new identifier, Content ID (CID) is proposed to make APCN fit for networks focusing on content delivery. CID can uniquely identify content, and it can also be used in content self-certifying. In addition, with the proposed CID, a content can be verified using any of its packets.
- A double-delegate paradigm with one remote delegate in the source network domain and one delegate in the local network domain is proposed in APCN. It can make full use of in-network cache in content-based networks to obtain the verification information from a nearby delegate.
- The proposed architecture allows built-in support on the privacy protection for both content senders and requesters, which also benefit from double-delegate paradigm.
- The potential security issues of the proposed APCN architecture in real-world deployment are analyzed, and the corresponding solutions are provided and discussed.

It should be noted that the content-based network considered in this chapter is an abstract network focused on content delivery. The proposed solution does not specifically target at a specific network technology or architecture (e.g., P2P or CDN) for content transmission. In other words, the proposed solution can be applied for the networks under a content-centric mode.

4.2 Application Scenarios

As we mentioned in Chap. 1, the proposed content-based architecture corresponds to the many-to-one communication mode. In a network with content transmission as the main requirement, one manifestation of the many-to-one mode is that after a content is sent by the sender, the content requester can obtain the content from multiple places, such as from the original sender or from intermediate nodes which have the cache of the content. In the architecture introduced in this chapter, the sender of the content plays an important role. In our design, if a content is sent by different senders, different content identifiers will be generated. Therefore, when we refer to the *same content* in this chapter, it means not only that the content itself is the same, but also that the content comes from the same sender. This is different from what is described in the ICN architecture [3, 9]. In this way, we can better locate and prevent the spread of malicious content. The architecture presented in this chapter will support this feature.

Another manifestation of the many-to-one mode is that when we need to verify whether a content has a certain source, we can verify and get the verification results from multiple places including the original network accountability domain and the local accountability domain. In other words, the verification process and the results of verification are not only available from the source accountability domain.

In the following, we provide two specific scenarios as examples.

Scenario 1. We consider a scenario where requesters want to send anonymous requests to obtain desired contents from the sender which might be a CP. To protect the privacy of the requester, the CP (possibly a sensitive site) hides the real address of the requester when sending the content back to the requester. In this process, we need to prevent malicious anonymous accesses to the CP and also the malicious CP (e.g., its servers are used to attack other network nodes). Consequently, the behaviors of both the requesters and the CP need to be checked. Considering that a requester is not located in the same accountability domain with the CP, if other requesters request the same content from the same domain as this requester, they can verify the validity of the content locally (e.g., verify whether the content is from an honest CP), without having to go to the CP's accountability domain for verification.

Scenario 2. We consider another simple scenario. When a user records an interesting video, and he wants to send the multimedia content to multiple people (e.g., his friends), we need a new architecture that can provide more efficient and greener services to balance accountability and privacy, e.g., generating verification information based on content rather than flow. In other words, we only need to generate one brief message per content, rather than generating one brief message for each receiver.

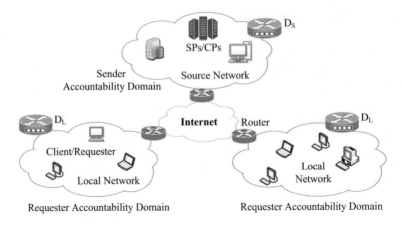

Fig. 4.1 The proposed APCN architecture with double delegates

4.3 Overview of the Architecture

We have introduced the independent third parties in Sect. 2.3.3. Generally, a third party can play a balancing role, which can be used to balance the rights and interests of the two peers with conflicting interests. In the APCN architecture, delegates act as a third party to balance privacy and accountability. The main purpose of using delegate is to achieve a balance between the needs of users for privacy protection and the needs of managers for behavior supervision. In addition, a delegate adopted in the source domain only is insufficient to achieve the goal of scalable accountability in large-scale content-based networks. That is because if verify requests for a content must be sent to the sender's delegate, lots of bandwidth resources will be required. Furthermore, if the distance between the source domain and the verifier who wants to challenge the received packet is relatively far, it will also cause a long delay in the transmission process.

Therefore, the proposed APCN includes the double accountability delegates shown in Fig. 4.1: a source delegate (D_S) in the sender accountability domain and a local delegate (D_L) in the requester accountability domain. D_S is responsible for the senders and hides the true identity of the senders if needed. This delegate cannot guarantee that the packet issued by the sender is correct or non-malicious but merely works as a third party to acknowledge whether the packet was truly issued by the sender. Attacks from senders can be prevented by the *Shutoff* procedure (more details on shutoff procedure is discussed in Sect. 4.4.3). To protect the privacy of the requesters and achieve the goal of enhancing network performance in terms of reducing packet delay, lowering bandwidth consumption, and decreasing access burden to the source delegate, D_L is proposed in the APCN architecture. D_L plays an important role in balancing accountability and privacy for requesters, and it caches the required information used to respond to the requests from local verifiers.

Table 4.1 Addresses in the packet header

Address type	Format	Note
Destination address	$NID_D : HID_D : CID_D$	Mandatory
Accountability address	$NID_A : HID_A : CID_A$	Mandatory
Return address	$NID_R : HID_R : CID_R$	Optional

In the following, we will describe the address used in APCN architecture and the process of requesting content. Then, we will introduce local delegate (D_L) in detail.

4.3.1 Addresses

The meaning of IP address has become overloaded, especially the source address represents too many roles in today's Internet [10]. To balance privacy and accountability, it is necessary to separate the packet accountability address and the return address originally integrated in the source address. A recent work [11] contributed to separating these two types of addresses in a packet-based scheme. However, its address format (including a Network ID, a Host ID and a Socket ID) is fundamentally unsuitable for content-based networks because it can only identify a flow, but cannot identify the same content sent by the same sender in different flows.

In the APCN architecture, each packet has three addresses: destination address, accountability address, and return address. Each address consists of three elements, i.e., a Network ID (NID) used to identify a network domain, a Host ID (HID) used to represent a host, and a Content ID (CID) used for the identification of different contents. Table 4.1 shows different types of addresses with their formats.

It is worth noting that, although the combination of NID and HID, i.e., NID:HID, can be used to locate a unique host, the CID is adopted for finer-grained positioning in a host. In other words, the CID can be used to distinguish different contents in the same host. The NID and HID are generated by the hash of their public keys, and the CID will be explained below.

In APCN, the CID is proposed as a key element for overcoming the limitations of the packet-based approach. There are three goals of using the CID, i.e., (1) it is capable of self-certifying; (2) it can effectively identify a content, where the same content issued from a sender to different requesters will have the identical identity, and the same content issued by different senders will have different identities; (3) it can meet the requirements of verifying a content based on any of its packets at any time instead of performing the verification after receiving all the packets of a content.

Considering the above-mentioned requirements for CID, it is not suitable for the proposed APCN architecture if the CID is a hash of the content. That is because if the CID is only generated by the hash of the content, the same content sent by different senders will have the same CID. Thus, we cannot distinguish who should be held accountable when needed. Therefore, in APCN the CID is more than just a simple hash of the content but also binds the public key of the sender and the address of the accountability delegate to the content, i.e.,

$$\text{CID} = H(Content \| K^{+}_{sender} \| (NID_A : HID_A))$$

where H is a cryptographically secure hash function, and $\|$ represents concatenation. The accountability delegate address $(NID_A : HID_A)$ is used to distinguish the same content sent from different accountability domains. K^{+}_{sender} is the public key of the sender and K^{-}_{sender} denotes the private key of the sender. K^{+}_{sender} is included in the CID to distinguish the same content issued by different senders in the same accountability domain. In addition, K^{+}_{sender} plays an important role in the self-certifying process [12, 13].

The CID is generated when the content is produced, and it can uniquely identify a content. When a content is divided into several packets for transmission, the same CID carried in the headers of these packets can be used to verify the corresponding content at any time, waiting for the entire content to be fully received.

Why is the CID designed to be self-certifying? As we introduced in Sect. 2.3.2, the self-certifying identifier has been considered as the trend in the development of communication networks [13–15]. Another important reason is that, although the delegate acting as a third party can vouch for a sender or a requester, i.e., the delegate can confirm that a requester issues a request or a sender sends a content. However, it is not possible for the delegate to verify that the sender owns the content. If someone needs to confirm that the sender is the owner of the content, the CID should have the ability of self-certifying. Therefore, in addition to NID and HID, CID as part of the address should also be self-certifying.

In APCN, the public/private key pair of the sender is allowed to be generated by the sender, and then the public key is sent to the accountability delegate. The key pair does not require frequent replacement, and the sender can decide when to regenerate a new key pair. If delegates find different senders having the same public key in the same accountability domain, they can ask these senders to regenerate a new key pair. Otherwise, the same content issued by different senders in this accountability domain would have the same CID.

In APCN, a pair of NID:HID (i.e., $NID_A : HID_A$ and $NID_D : HID_D$) can be used to identify a network flow[1], and the CID can be used to distinguish different contents in a flow. When a sender sends the same content to different receivers, the CID might appear in different flows. This allows APCN to locate the problem more accurately. For example, when we want to stop forwarding malicious or illegal content, we can shutoff a content transmission rather than a flow, unless the sender is an attacker (more details on shutoff will be discussed in Sect. 4.4.3).

---

[1] According to RFC 6437 [16], a *network flow* is a sequence of packets sent from a particular source (sender) to a particular destination (receiver) that the source desires to label as a flow. We follow this definition in this book.

With the newly introduced flexible content identifier proposed in this chapter, the same content issued from the same sender to different requesters would have the identical identity, and the same content issued by different senders would have different identities.

4.3.2   The Request Process

The lifecycle of the request process in APCN is shown in Fig. 4.2, including the following steps:

1. The requester issues a request to the sender who has the content. In this process, an accountability address will be carried with the role of source address to prevent intermediate routers from knowing the requester's real source address. If required, the requester's source address can be encrypted and sent to the content provider (sender) along with the payload of the data packet.
2. The requester sends the brief message to D_L, where the brief message is used to verify what the sender has issued (more details on brief messaging is discussed in Sect. 4.4.1).
3. A verifier can challenge any request sent by requesters. The sender and any intermediate nodes (e.g., routers) along the path can be the verifier. More details on the verification process are discussed in Sect. 4.4.2. If the sender determines that the request it received is malicious or illegal, it can stop verifying this request by notifying the delegate, and the delegate will punish the requester if required (more details on the shutoff process are discussed in Sect. 4.4.3).
4. If the requester allows the sender to know its true identity, the sender can use the requester's source address, which has been encrypted, in the payload for response or connection purposes. In this process, content producers (e.g., users who generate the content) or CPs (e.g., data centers) can act as the sender. Since the content has been encrypted, intermediate nodes still never know what the requester has requested.
5. If the requester does not provide its true identity in the payload, the sender responds to the request with the requester's accountability address (the address of D_L). After receiving the content, D_L forwards it to the requester. This approach is an alternative option to Step 4 and can be used to mitigate the traffic analysis attack.
6. Similar to Step 2, the sender issues the brief message to D_S. The purpose of this design is to ensure that the behavior of the sender can also be effectively constrained.
7. A verifier can challenge a content issued by the sender through verifying any packet of that content (rather than after receiving all the packets of the content). Similar to Step 3, the verify and shutoff processes may occur during content transmission. In general, the verification request is directed to D_L and then forwarded to D_S only when the verification cannot be performed at D_L. More details

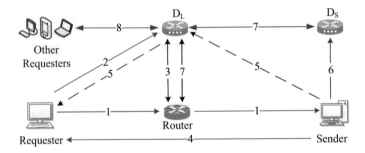

Fig. 4.2 The lifecycle of the request process in the proposed APCN architecture

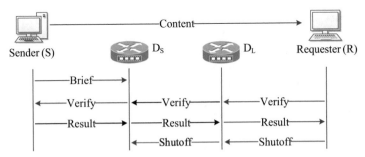

Fig. 4.3 An overview of the request process

on the verify and shutoff procedures are discussed in Sect. 4.4.2 and Sect. 4.4.3, respectively.

8. In some networks, if D_L or the local network caches the content (perhaps the requester's neighbor nodes have requested the content), the requester can directly obtain the content from the local network, and then we can still follow Steps 1-5 to take the accountability of the original sender at the local network. It should be noted that, if a content comes from different senders, each sender needs to be vouched.

Figure 4.3 shows an overview of the request process. Given that the Internet is divided into many geographical network domains, the design of the APCN architecture can efficiently achieve a scalable balance of accountability and privacy in large-scale content-based networks.

4.3.3 Local Delegate (D_L)

As we have described in the *lifecycle of the request process*, local delegate (D_L) plays an important role in balancing the privacy and accountability of the requester (see Fig. 4.2).

Table 4.2 Cached information in D_L used for local packet verifying

Content ID (CID)	Validation result (T/F)	Expiration time (s)
CID1	T	10
CID2	F	25
CID3	T	30

In addition, D_L is another key element in the proposed APCN architecture, which is used to reduce the delay of packet verification through local verifying. The verification information stored in D_L includes the CID, the results of the verification and the expiration time. A typical example of what is stored in D_L can be found in Table 4.2. "T/F" can be used to indicate the validation result to denote whether a delegate vouches for a packet (content). Since we do not add a synchronization or push mechanism between D_L and D_S, for security considerations, we set the expiration time for each entry in D_L [17]. The purpose of this design is that we can make decisions as soon as we have the result for the change of a content (e.g., a content changes from normal content to harmful content). Therefore, the expiration time can also help decrease the negative effects when the requester cannot detect the malicious problem in time. After the expiration time, the verification information needs to be re-acquired from D_S (this is elaborated in Sect. 4.4.2). The setting of the expiration time is discussed in Sect. 4.7.1.

The storage occupied by the cached verification information is another factor required in the proposed design. If there is not enough storage space, the entry (cached verification information) will be removed by a suitable replacement policy, e.g., Least Recently Used (LRU).

In contrast to the existing work focusing only on the protection of sender privacy, this design (i.e., double-delegate paradigm with one remote delegate in the source network domain and one delegate in the local network domain) allows the proposed architecture to include built-in support on the privacy protection for both content senders and requesters. In addition, this design is able to enhance network performance by verifying packets via the delegate at the local network, reducing the packet transmission delay, lowering bandwidth consumption, and decreasing the access burden to the original remote delegate.

4.4 The Accountability Process

This section will introduce how to perform accountability in APCN. In the following, let $\{x\}_{KEY}$ indicate a signature on x with a KEY. The KEY can be a private key or a symmetric key. For example, $\{x\}_{K_A^-}$ denotes a signature on x with A's private key and $\{x\}_{K_{AB}}$ represents a signature on x with a symmetric key shared by A and B. Let $\rightarrow$ represent the packet transmission path, e.g., $A \rightarrow B$ indicates packets sent from

A to *B*. To make it clearer, the following abbreviations will be used throughout this section: *S* denotes the Sender, *R* represents the Requester, *V* indicates Verifier, *P* is the Packet, *H* is the cryptographically secured hash function, and MAC denotes the Message Authentication Code.

4.4.1   Send Brief Message

In this process, *S* sends a brief message to D_S to notify what it has issued. The brief message needs to contain enough information to allow D_S to respond to any verification request for user's behavior. Each brief message includes a Client ID, a fingerprint and a MAC using the key K_{SD_S}:

$$\text{Brief}(P) = Client\ ID \| F(P) \| MAC_{K_{SD_S}}(Client\ ID \| F(P))$$

where *Client ID* is used to notify D_S who sent the packet. It could be either the sender's HID or other identifiers only known by D_S. In Sect. 2.3.3, we have introduced how to manage the user's identity if the Client ID is not a fixed identifier (e.g., an HID) of the user. MAC is a tool used to ensure message integrity. The fingerprint is used as the evidence to respond to the verification request. D_S stores fingerprints and determines whether the content was truly sent by *S* through querying whether the corresponding fingerprint exists. The packet fingerprint *F(P)* is given by

$$F(P) = H(K_{SD_S} \| CID \| H(P_{body}))$$

where K_{SD_S} is a symmetric key which is only known by *S* and D_S. K_{SD_S} will be created if D_S agrees to vouch for *S*, and the K_{SD_S} can be replaced periodically. K_{SD_S} is included in the fingerprint to prevent others from establishing the association between *P* and *F(P)*. Because if the relationship between *P* and *F(P)* is established, the user's behavior can be obtained indirectly. Therefore, it is also a measure to protect the privacy of the senders. P_{body} represents the payload of a packet. It is included in the *F(P)* to meet the requirement of verifying a content at any time based on any packet belonging to that content.

Instead of sending full-size fingerprints, a bloom filter can be used. Specifically, *S* can periodically send a bloom filter to D_S after collecting fingerprints. In this case, K_{SD_S} is no longer needed in the fingerprint, because if we use a bloom filter, it is difficult for an observer (e.g., an malicious network user) to know what is contained in the fingerprint. An observer will not infer user's behavior (e.g., which user is issuing contents) by analyzing brief messages and the packets forwarded in the network. The use of a bloom filter can reduce the storage usage of D_S and the network overhead (especially the overhead of bandwidth resources) between *S* and D_S, but at the same time, the false positive rate of the bloom filter is inevitable. It is worth noting that, regardless of whether the direct transmission of fingerprints or bloom filters is used, the delegate will not know the payload of the content issued by the sender.

4.4.2 Check User's Behavior

The process of checking user behavior is called the verification process. In this process, the verifier can check whether a delegate is responsible for a content. A verifier can check any received packets belonging to a content. After receiving the request for verification, the delegate will check two things: (1) whether the content was truly sent by S through checking whether the corresponding fingerprint exists in D_S or the corresponding CID exists in D_L, and (2) the transmission (forwarding) of this content has not been stopped. If both checks are passed, the delegate replies with a VERIFIED message. It is worth noting that only one packet of the same content is required to be verified because all packets of a content carry the same CID in their headers. Once validated, the verifier can maintain a whitelist locally for recording which CID (corresponding to a content) has recently been verified. We can set a duration to keep this whitelist alive. After the valid time has expired, the verifier needs to check the user's behavior again to avoid some cases, e.g., the sender is attacked during this period of time, or a content is found to be malicious or illegal after being reported but has not been detected before.

In our proposal, a verifier only needs to verify a single packet from a content, and then it whitelists all other packets with the same CID. How can we stop an attacker from using this CID to send arbitrary packets? Because the brief message sent by the user to the delegate includes the hash of packets (see Sect. 4.4.1), the verifier can use any packet of the content to challenge the sender. If an attacker steals the CID, the payload of the fake packet will be incorrect. If the fake packet is used in the verification process, it will not pass the verify. If the CID is stolen, but the fake packet is not issued to the delegate for verification, even if the requester receives the packet, it still cannot be used to assemble the content, and the requester will require the packet to be retransmitted.

When a verifier checks a network user's behavior, the following three cases may occur.

4.4.2.1 No Validation Results Found at the Local Delegate

A verifier first enquires whether D_L has a record of verification results of a content. If no result could be found because that content has not been requested or verified locally or the content verification result stored locally has expired, D_L will forward the request to D_S.

4.4.2.2 Validation Results Found at the Local Delegate

When the verification response by D_S returns, D_L caches the result. If other verifiers in the same accountability domain need to verify the same content, the verification is performed directly by D_L. This greatly improves the efficiency of verification and reduces the consumption of network resources.

4.4.2.3   No Verification Information in the Delegate

If information used for verification cannot be found in all delegates (including D_S and D_L), because the verification information is expired, or the brief messages and validation results are lost during transmission, we can obtain the results from the sender. In this case, D_S can send a verification request to the sender. The sender verifies whether the content was sent by itself. If the sender does not support recursive verification in this form, or cannot confirm whether the content was sent by itself, because there might be no record in the sender or the sender has re-generated the corresponding CID, the content is not vouched for by any delegate. In this case, we can consider that the source of the content is unknown, and the content needs to be dropped. Then, the requester can re-request the content.

In real-world deployment, these three cases usually occur sequentially. However, if the verifier and the sender are in the same accountability domain and they use the same delegate, then the D_L and D_S are actually the same delegate. Therefore, even if the local delegate has no verification result, the verify request will not be forwarded. It should be noted that the verifier does not know whether the verify request is forwarded. As a result, the verifier cannot know whether it is in the same accountability domain as the sender.

When a verifier sends the verify request to the delegate, it needs to include the CID and the hash of the packet. MAC with K_V is used to ensure that the response from the delegate is what V requests, where K_V is the private key only known by the verifier V. This process can be expressed as

$$V \rightarrow D_L \text{ and } D_L \rightarrow D_S :$$
$$\text{Verify}(P) = CID \| H(P_{body}) \| MAC_{K_V}(CID \| H(P_{body}))$$

If there is no verification information in the delegate, D_S sends the verification to the sender, i.e.,

$$D_S \rightarrow S : \{ VERIFICATION \| CID \}_{K_{SD_S}}$$

where the *VERIFICATION* is the request sent from D_S to S. After obtaining the verification result, the delegate will respond to the verifier through the following processes.

$$D_S \rightarrow D_L \text{ and } D_L \rightarrow V :$$
$$\text{Result}(P) = \{ VERIFIED \| \text{Verify}(P) \}_{K_{D_S}^-}$$

where $K_{D_S}^+/K_{D_S}^-$ is the public/private key pair of D_S.

4.4.3 *Stop Malicious Behavior*

When a receiver (i.e., a sender or a requester) identifies a malicious behavior, it can send a shutoff message as an instruction to stop the traffic. The process of issuing a shutoff message is similar to the verification process. The shutoff message will first be sent to D_L, then it will be forwarded to D_S, i.e.,

$$V \rightarrow D_L :$$
$$\text{Shutoff}(P)_{D_L} = \{CID\|H(P_{body})\|duration\}_{K_R^-}$$
$$D_L \rightarrow D_S :$$
$$\text{Shutoff}(P)_{D_S} = \{CID\|H(P_{body})\|duration\|HID_V\}_{K_{D_L}^-}$$

where the *duration* is the length of time that the delegate stops verifying the content sent from the malicious sender. The HID_V is the HID of the verifier who sends the shutoff, which should be carried by the shutoff message when being forwarded from D_L to D_S. This is because if malicious shutoff messages are detected, the one who sent the shutoff message could be accountable through D_L. Therefore, D_L also records the shutoff requests. The recorded information can be used in subsequent actions to investigate malicious shutoff messages.

What should be done when a sender's delegate receives a shutoff message for a particular CID? Should the sender's delegate block all future transmissions of that piece of content or all future transmissions from that sender? Our suggestion is to make different decisions based on different situations. Delegates can record and count the number of valid shutoff messages. For an occasional case, e.g., only one requester sends a shutoff message against the content, we can stop the content being forwarded to the requester who sent the shutoff message. If a content is reported as malicious by many requesters, we can stop forwarding that content in the network. When a sender issues considerable malicious contents, it is necessary to prevent the sender from sending packets for a period of time and even address the sender's legal responsibilities.

4.4.4 *Forwarding Processes*

Many studies have focused on improving the flexibility of the network. Overlay networks [18, 19] is one of them, and it has been widely advocated. However, the overlay-to-underlay mapping will result in inefficiencies [20]. There has been some proposed new architectures having different address formats and packet headers with those in the current Internet to solve the problem of such inefficiencies [20, 21].

In the proposed APCN architecture, the forwarding process can be performed according to the packet header (i.e., addresses) without the need of encapsulation for tunnelling or other process (e.g., mapping of overlay-to-underlay). Figure 4.4 shows

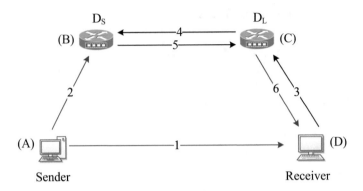

Fig. 4.4 The basic forwarding process of the proposed APCN architecture

the basic forwarding process of the proposed APCN architecture, which is a sim-
plified version of Fig. 4.2. Specifically, the process depicted in Fig. 4.4 is applicable
to both the process of requesting content and the process of sending content. Correspondingly, Fig. 4.2 shows the whole process. For example, when the requester issues
a request to the content owner, the sender in Fig. 4.4 is the requester in Fig. 4.2, and
the receiver, i.e., the content owner is the sender in Fig. 4.2. The detailed illustration
is shown in Table 4.3, where we use Nodes A, B, C and D to represent Sender, Source
Delegate (D_S), Local Delegate (D_L), and Receiver, respectively.

Because there are three addresses in the packet header, in addition to referring
to different identities (i.e., destination address, accountability address and return
address), they can also do more when forwarding packets. When delegates or routers
receive the packet, they will follow the rules that *the accountability address can be
considered as the next destination address after the packet arrives at the destination.* Return address indicates where the packet should be sent to after reaching the
accountability address. In practical deployment, we do not need to make any changes
to the existing routers. After receiving packets, the delegate forwards packets based
on the packet header according to the rules.

4.5 Theoretical Analysis

In this section, we analyze the efficiency of APCN compared to a packet-based (PKT)
architecture through theoretical analysis. In APCN, multiple requesters can use the
same validation information when acquiring the same content. This means that the
proposed APCN architecture can detect problems early, and then perform shutoff
or accountability actions. In addition, through theoretical analysis, it can be found
that APCN can reduce the RTT of packet verification and relieve the access burden
to the delegate D_S. Figure 4.5 shows the difference in the accountability processes
between APCN and PKT architectures.

Table 4.3 The packet header used in different forwarding processes

Process	Address type	Node	Address
Send packet	Destination	D	$NID_D : HID_D : CID_D$
$A \rightarrow D$	Accountability	B	$NID_B : HID_B : CID_B$
	Return	N/A	N/A
Send brief	Destination	B	$NID_B : HID_B : CID_B$
$A \rightarrow B$	Accountability	A	$NID_A : HID_A : CID_A$
	Return	N/A	N/A
Verify/Shutoff	Destination	C	$NID_C : HID_C : CID_C$
$D \rightarrow C$	Accountability	B	$NID_B : HID_B : CID_B$
	Return	D	$NID_D : HID_D : CID_D$
Verify/Shutoff	Destination	B	$NID_B : HID_B : CID_B$
$C \rightarrow B$	Accountability	C	$NID_C : HID_C : CID_C$
	Return	D	$NID_D : HID_D : CID_D$
Return result	Destination	C	$NID_C : HID_C : CID_C$
$B \rightarrow C$	Accountability	D	$NID_D : HID_D : CID_D$
	Return	B	$NID_B : HID_B : CID_B$
Return result	Destination	D	$NID_D : HID_D : CID_D$
$C \rightarrow D$	Accountability	C	$NID_C : HID_C : CID_C$
	Return	B	$NID_B : HID_B : CID_B$

4.5.1 The Delay in the Verification Process

The delay of the verification process in the PKT architecture can be expressed as

$$D^{PKT} = \sum_{i \in V} R_{D_S,i} P_{D_S}$$

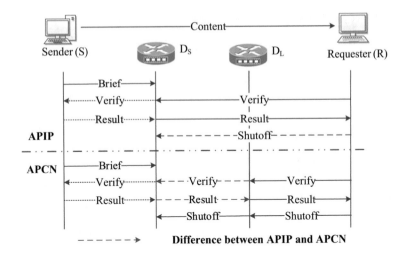

Fig. 4.5 The comparison of accountability process between APCN and PKT architectures

where $R_{D_S,i}$ denotes the RTT between the i-th verifier and D_S, and P_{D_S} is the probability of finding the verification information at D_S. V represents the set of verifiers.

In APCN, if the verification information is cached in D_L, the delay can be given by

$$D_{D_L}^{APCN} = \sum_{i \in V} R_{D_L,i} P_{D_L}$$

where $R_{D_L,i}$ denotes the RTT between the i-th verifier and D_L, and P_{D_L} is the probability of finding the verification information at D_L. If no verification information is found in D_L, the delay will be:

$$D_{D_S}^{APCN} = \sum_{i \in V} R_{D_S,i}(1 - P_{D_L})P_{D_S}, (R_{D_S,i} \geq R_{D_L,i})$$

and the reduced RTT can be given by

$$\Delta_{D^{APCN}} = \sum_{i \in V} R_{D_L,i} P_{D_L} - \sum_{i \in V} R_{D_S,i} P_{D_L} P_{D_S}$$

4.5.2 Reduced Access Burden to the Source Delegate

Let N_{total} denote the total number of requests (including verify requests and shutoff requests), and N_{D_L} represent the number of requests received at D_L. With the proposed APCN, the cache hit rate of D_S can be reduced by

$$\varphi = \frac{N_{total} - N_{D_L}}{N_{total}} = \frac{\sum_{j \in Q} Req_j (1 - P_{D_L})}{\sum_{j \in Q} Req_j} = 1 - P_{D_L}$$

where Q represents the set of requests, and Req_j denotes the j-th request issued by users (including verifiers and victims who sent the shutoff instructions).

4.5.3 Analysis of Space Complexity

Using the proposed APCN architecture, the maximum communication overhead, which involves verification information delivery, is no more than $Total_{message}(\Delta t)$:

$$Total_{message}(\Delta t) = m \times n \times (\delta + \delta) = 2mn\delta$$

where m represents the number of requesters (network users), and n denotes the request rate of a requester. δ denotes the cost of storing a piece of verification information in a given time window (Δt). Since there are two delegates in the accountability process (i.e., D_L and D_S), and each of them needs to store one copy, therefore two δ are needed. The space complexity of the PKT architecture is $mn\delta$ because the verification information in the PKT architecture only needs to be stored in the D_S.

4.5.4 Analysis of Time Complexity

In the proposed APCN architecture, the worst scenario is that there is no verification information in both D_L and D_S, and the verify message needs to be sent to the sender for verification (more details of this process can be found in Sect. 4.4.2.3). Therefore, the total time complexity of the accountability process in a given time window (Δt) is no more than $Total_{time}(\Delta t)$:

$$Total_{time}(\Delta t) = O(n^3)$$

However, in most cases, verifiers can obtain the verification results from the D_L (Sect. 4.7 addresses this argument). Even if the verifier needs to obtain the verification result from D_S, the time complexity is $O(n^2)$. The time complexity of the PKT architecture is $O(n^2)$. Because in the PKT architecture, verification information is sent directly to the D_S, and then sent to the sender if there is no result in the D_S.

4.6   Security Analysis and Countermeasures

In this section, a list of possible security problems that may be encountered in the real-world deployment of the proposed architecture and their countermeasures are analysed.

Threat Model. In the proposed architecture, threats may come from the sender, the verifier (intermediate routers or the receiver), and the content requester. Specifically, the sender might send malicious content to the requester or attack other network nodes. The verifier may send a large number of invalid and malicious verify requests. The requester may attack other network nodes by issuing a large number of malicious requests or sending a large number of invalid brief messages to the delegate. The intermediate node may initiate a replay attack using some packets of a content and the corresponding CID. Therefore, security threats may appear in the brief, verify and shutoff processes. The attack type includes DDoS attacks, flood attacks, replay attacks, and identity theft.

4.6.1   Attacks and Countermeasures in the Accountability Process

How to detect malicious behaviors in the brief process. In the process of sending brief messages, malicious users may send a flood of brief messages to their delegates. The delegate can take some policies to prevent such attacks. For example, a delegate can ask senders to use bloom filters when they send brief messages, or specify the maximum number of brief messages received per second from the same host. This flooding behavior can be detected. For example, a delegate receives numerous brief messages from a sender, but there is no verification request sent to the delegate to verify whether the sender has sent something.

How to deal with a large number of verification requests in which attacks may occur. In this process, delegates can count the source of the verification requests. If a verifier sends a large number of duplicate verify messages (ignoring the verification interval set by the delegate) over a period of time, the delegate will temporarily stop the verification request from that verifier. In addition, if a verifier sends a large number of invalid verification requests, e.g., the received verification cannot find the corresponding sender in the records, delegates will check whether the verifier is malicious or there are malicious nodes posing as a sender in the accountability domain.

Whether to respond to the shutoff instruction. Whether the delegate responds to the shutoff instruction is optional. Our suggestion is that if the shutoff is successful, the delegate can respond to the reporter who sent the shutoff message. Otherwise, the delegate can ignore such an instruction, or punish the verifier who sent malicious shutoff messages. If the verifier does not receive a response within the expected time, for example, due to the loss of shutoff messages during transmission, it can resend the shutoff message to the delegate.

4.6.2 The Security of the Content ID (CID)

We have described why CID is designed to be self-certifying in Sect. 4.3.1. Self-certifying means that an entity (e.g., a requester or a sender) claims to have an identity (e.g., CID), and other entities can verify whether the identity belongs to the claimant without the participation of a third party. That is because the sender's public key and the address of the delegate are available[2], anyone can verify the authenticity of the CID after receiving the content. In addition, if a node disguises the sender, it can also be discovered by the following steps:

1. The verifier sends a random nonce N to the one that declares itself to be the sender (requester or content owner).
2. The sender encrypts the random nonce N using its private key, and then sends the encrypted N along with its public key to the verifier if the verifier does not have the public key.
3. The verifier decrypts the encrypted random number N using the public key and determines whether the random number N is what it has sent to the sender.

The verifier can then calculate whether the hash of the content, the sender's public key and the delegate's address are equal to the CID, i.e., $H(Content \| K^+_{sender} \| (NID_A : HID_A)) = $ CID. In this process, the content is what the verifier receives, the accountability address (i.e., $NID_A : HID_A$) is in the packet header.

4.6.3 Leaking Privacy by Logs

The proposed APCN architecture can effectively mitigate the leakage of user privacy due to logs. That is because when a requester sends a request to a sender (i.e., the content owner), the source address in the packet header is the requester's account-ability address (i.e., requester's delegate address). Therefore, unless there is only one node in each accountability domain, log analysis can only learn that there is communication between two accountability domains, without learning which node makes the communication.

---

[2]The address of the delegate does not belong to the scope of privacy protection and is known to the public.

4.6.4   How to Deal with a Replay Attack

In the existing packet-based architecture [11], a fingerprint is a function of the sender, the receiver, and the data, while in APCN the fingerprint only depends on the sender and the data. Once a sender sends a brief message of a particular piece of content to its delegate, an attacker might replay any packet from that content to other nodes in the network. In this case, the victim sends a shutoff message to inform the local delegate which CID has been used by the attacker. Because the shutoff message is sent to the local delegate in the first instance (then forwarded to the source delegate), when subsequent packets of the content used for attacks enter the local accountability domain, the delegate will stop vouching for that content, and the routers stop forwarding that content. In this way, the attack will be blocked. It is worth noting that shutoff does not affect the normal communication of both sides, i.e., the sender can still transmit other contents to the requester. However, in the existing packet-based architecture, if the receiver (e.g., content requester) sends a shutoff message to the sender's delegate, the other packets from the sender to the receiver (i.e., the specific flow) will be blocked. As a result, the sender will not be able to send other contents to the receiver for a period of time. In other words, it will affect the normal transmission of other contents, especially when a flow contains multiple contents.

4.7   Performance Evaluation

In this section, we conduct extensive experiments to validate the effectiveness of the proposed APCN architecture and evaluate its performance. In particular, we compare the performance of APCN with that of the packet-based (PKT) architecture [11] to show its relative merits. To achieve this purpose, we develop a discrete-event simulator based on the NS-3 simulation framework [22] and implement both the APCN and the PKT architectures. Table 4.4 shows the key system parameters.

The system parameters are set based on the existing studies [2, 23] and real-world measurements. The dataset comes from a SIGCOMM paper [2], which contains more than 100,000 objects, and the request rate distribution follows Zipf's law [24]. Given that the exponent parameter of the Zipf distribution is 0.99 in the United States, 0.92 in Europe, and 1.04 in Asia [2], in this section, we chose 1.0 as the default value.

The same topology used in Fig. 4.2 is adopted in the simulation environment. The topology of the China Science and Technology Network (CSTNET), a small ISP with more than 400 nodes is used to simulate the local network. A core router of CSTNET is selected as D_L, and the 345 leaf routers act as requesters.

The hop count and link delay between D_S and D_L can reflect the distance between them. To have reasonable settings of link variables (e.g., delay), we made some real-world measurements. A measurement result reveals that the RTT between Beijing and a site in the Henan University (HENU) in Kaifeng that is approximately 600 km away from Beijing is 32 ms. Another measurement result shows that the RTT

Table 4.4 The parameters setting

Parameter	Value
Number of requesters	345
Link delay between D_S and D_L	3 ms/hop $\times$ 10 hops = 30 ms
Replacement	Least Recently Used (LRU)
Payload	1,024 Bytes
Link bandwidth at local networks	100 Mbps
Link bandwidth between D_S and D_L	1,000 Mbps
Max packets for transmission queue on the link (both directions)	10,000 packets
Number of content	100,000
Cache size in delegates	100,000 packets
Expiration time of verification information	30 s
Link delay of connections at local networks (link delay between nodes)	1 ms
The request rate	100 requests/s
Request packet size	31 Bytes
Zipf (q, α)	(0, 1.0)
Simulation time	600 s

between Beijing and a farther site in Hong Kong is 169 ms. Based on these results, the delay between D_S and D_L is initially set to 30 ms. The effects of varying distances between D_S and D_L are evaluated in Sect. 4.7.7.

We conduct experiments to investigate the effects of different settings of the expiration time of the verification information stored in the delegate on network performance. We find that with the expiration time exceeding 30 s, the network performance will not have significant improvement (see Sect. 4.7.1). Therefore, the expiration time of verification information in D_L is set to 30 s in the simulation.

To evaluate the effect of different parameters on performance, we change the number of content from 10,000 to 60,000 in Sect. 4.7.2 and set α (Zipf distribution parameter) from 0.7 to 1.3 in Sect. 4.7.3. In Sect. 4.7.4, we vary the cache size in the delegate. We increase the request rate of the requesters from 25 to 150 in Sect. 4.7.5. In Sect. 4.7.6, we vary the number of requesters. In Sect. 4.7.7, we change the distance between D_S and D_L by changing the link delay. The default parameters are shown in Table 4.4. In each subsection, we will list the main parameters in a smaller table and mark the changed parameters and the changes of their values. If a parameter is not listed in the tables in subsections, it means that it has not changed, and its value can be found in Table 4.4.

Two key performance metrics are adopted to evaluate the performance of these architectures: reduced RTT ratio and cache hit rate. The *reduced RTT ratio* represents the effect of the reduced RTT in the accountability process when using the proposed APCN compared with that when using the PKT architecture. The *cache hit rate* is the probability of successfully finding the verification information at D_L, reflecting the effect of reducing the burden of accessing D_S and reducing the bandwidth consumption between D_L and D_S. These two performance metrics can be expressed as follows:

$$Reduced\ RTT\ Ratio = \frac{\overline{RTT}_{pkt} - \overline{RTT}_{apcn}}{\overline{RTT}_{pkt}}$$

$$Cache\ Hit\ Rate = \frac{N_{hit}}{N_{hit} + N_{miss}}$$

where $\overline{RTT}_{pkt}$ and $\overline{RTT}_{apcn}$ are the average RTTs for the accountability process under the PKT and the APCN architectures, respectively. N_{hit} is the number of packets successfully verified at D_L, and N_{miss} is the number of packets that do not find the verification information at D_L.

4.7.1   Effects of the Expiration Time of Verification Information Cached in the Delegates

If an entry of verification information is cached in the delegate for a short period of time, many verification results need to be retrieved from the D_S. In principle, the longer the valid time of the verification information, the more verification requests will be served by the cached verification information. However, if the valid time is set too long, when a content is re-identified as malicious content from normal content, the system will not be able to change the cached verification information in time. This will be detrimental to the security of the network. In addition, if the verification information is cached by delegate for too long, it will take up a lot of storage space. In the meantime, a popular content may become an unpopular content, and people no longer frequently request the content, so the corresponding verification information does not need to be stored for a long time. Therefore, there are many factors that need to be considered in the setting of the expiration time of verification information. Setting the expiration time that is too long or too short is not good for the network managers and network users.

To investigate the effects of the expiration time of the cached entries in the delegate, we change the expiration time from 10 to 60 ms. The parameters in this section are shown in Table 4.5. Figure 4.6 depicts the performance results between APCN and the PKT architectures against the varying expiration time under different numbers of contents.

Figure 4.6a shows the reduced RTT ratio (recall that the reduced RTT ratio reflects the performance improvement due to the use of APCN compared with the PKT architecture), and Fig. 4.6b depicts the cache hit rate of D_L, which reflects the effect of relieving the access burden on D_S.

Table 4.5 The parameters in the evaluation of the expiration time

Parameter	Value
Number of requesters	345
Link delay between D_S and D_L	30 ms
Number of content	100,000, 200,000, 300,000
Cache size in delegates	100,000, 200,000, 300,000
	Consistent with the number of content
Expiration time of verification information	*Increase from 10, 20, 30, 40, 50 to 60 s*
The request rate	100 requests/s
Zipf (q, α)	(0, 1.0)

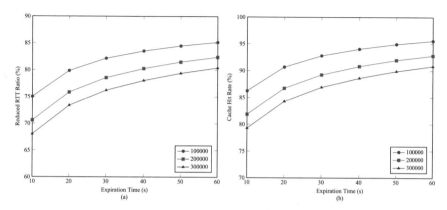

Fig. 4.6 Effects of expiration time of cache entry in delegates: **a** reduced RTT ratio and **b** cache hit rate

From this figure, we find that with the increase in the expiration time, the network performance improves, since both the reduced RTT ratio and the cache hit rate increase. The increase in the cache hit rate means that more verify() procedures are performed at the local delegate, D_L, resulting in reduced access to the source delegate, D_S. As the number of content increases, the network performance degrades. We will explain this phenomenon and discuss the effects of the number of content in Sect. 4.7.2. From Fig. 4.6, we also find that, when the expiration time increases, the performance improvement due to the use of APCN slows down, especially when the expiration time exceeds 30 s. This is because with the growth of the expiration time, the frequency of retrieving verification information from D_S is reduced, i.e., the negative effects of the expiration time are gradually reduced.

In actual deployment, the system can pre-determine and continuously adjust the expiration time of the verification information based on various factors such as the storage and computing capabilities of the network equipment, whether the network environment is secure or trusted, and the frequency of network attacks.

Table 4.6 The parameters in the evaluation of the number of content

Parameter	Value
Number of requesters	345
Link delay between D_S and D_L	30 ms
Number of content	*Increase from 100,000, 200,000, 300,000, 400,000, 500,000 to 600,000*
Cache size in delegates	Consistent with the number of content
Expiration time of verification information	30 s
The request rate	100 requests/s
Zipf (q, α)	(0, 1.0)

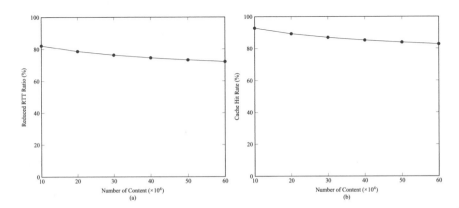

Fig. 4.7 Effects of the number of content: **a** reduced RTT ratio and **b** cache hit rate

4.7.2   Effects of the Number of Content

In Sect. 4.7.1, we compared the effects of the expiration time of the cache entry under different numbers of content (i.e., 100,000, 200,000 and 300,000). We can observe a slight decrease in the network performance when the number of content increases. To evaluate the effect of the number of content, Fig. 4.7 shows the performance metrics against the varying number of content from 100,000 to 600,000. The other parameters are unchanged and are the default values (see Table 4.6 for detailed parameters setting).

In the Fig. 4.7, we can see that with the increase in the number of content, the performance of APCN compared with the PKT architecture has significant improvement. For example, when the number of content is 300,000, the reduced RTT ratio is 76.19%, and the cache hit rate in the D_L is 86.92%. In addition, the effect of performance improvement due to the use of APCN is gradually reduced. Specifically, when the number of content increases from 100,000 to 600,000, the reduced RTT ratio drops from 82.14 to 72.10%, and the cache hit rate drops from 92.80 to 82.82%.

This phenomenon is because as the increase in the number of content, the number of times accessing D_S to obtain the verification information also increases.

The evaluation results in this section mean that compared to the PKT architecture, the performance of the proposed APCN will be significantly improved, but the effect of the performance improvement will gradually decrease if the number of content increases. In reality, with the increase in the number of content, the number of users (requesters) and the request rate also grow rapidly [6]. The merits of the proposed APCN architecture are more apparent if the user's request rate or the number of users increases (see Sects. 4.7.5 and 4.7.6).

4.7.3 Effects of the Content Popularity

In this section, we consider the Zipf distribution for content popularity, as it has been widely used in related studies for this purpose [25]. The content popularity is reflected in different distributions of the content request. In the Zipf distribution, q denotes the parameter of rank, and α represents the value of the exponent characterizing the distribution. To investigate the effects of content popularity, we set the parameters of the Zipf distribution as follows: $q = 0$ and $\alpha = 0.7, 0.8, 0.9, 1.0, 1.1, 1.2$ and 1.3. With $q = 0$, the increase in α shows the increase in the concentration of the request. The detailed parameters setting is shown in Table 4.7.

Figure 4.8 shows the improvement of APCN compared with the PKT architecture against the varying α. From this figure, we can find that with the increase in the parameter α, both the reduced RTT ratio and the cache hit rate increase. In other words, the performance of the APCN architecture improves as the parameter α increases. Specifically, as the value of α increases from 0.7 to 1.3, the reduced RTT ratio increases from 83.03 to 84.76%, and the cache hit rate in D_L increases from 91.26 to 96.29%. This is because more verify requests can be performed at D_L in the local network before the verification information expires. In other words, the accountability for those contents is promptly verified locally. In the real world, the

Table 4.7 The parameters in the evaluation of the content popularity

Parameter	Value
Number of requesters	345
Link delay between D_S and D_L	30 ms
Number of content	100,000
Cache size in delegates	100,000
Expiration time of verification information	30 s
The request rate	100 requests/s
Zipf (q, α)	*(0, 0.7), (0, 0.8), (0, 0.9), (0, 1.0), (0, 1.1), (0, 1.2), (0, 1.3)*

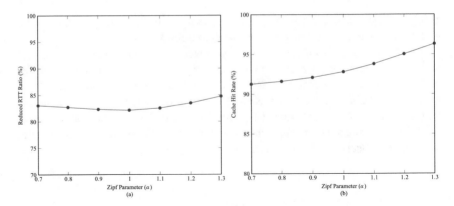

Fig. 4.8 Effects of content popularity: **a** reduced RTT ratio and **b** cache hit rate

higher the popularity of the content, the higher the frequency and the larger number of verification requests that are processed at D_L.

4.7.4 Effects of the Delegate Cache Ability

In this section, we change the cache size in the delegates to assess the impact of caching ability on network performance. The cache ability is defined as follows:

$$Cache\ Ability = \frac{S_{cache}}{N_{content}}$$

where S_{cache} represents the cache size in the delegates, and $N_{content}$ denotes the number of content. The parameters of this evaluation are shown in Table 4.8 and the evaluation results can be found in Fig. 4.9.

From Fig. 4.9 we can see that when the cache ability reaches 90%, the growth of the cache ability does not affect the performance improvement. In fact, when the cache ability exceeds 60%, the increase in cache ability has a limited impact on performance improvement. This view can be confirmed by the evaluation results. When the cache ability increases from 60 to 100%, the reduced RTT ratio increases from 81.10 to 82.14%, and the cache hit rate goes up from 91.84 to 92.80%. In other words, when the cache ability reaches a certain level, increasing the cache ability will have limited performance improvement in the APCN architecture. That is because under the current parameters setting, if the cache ability is less than 90%, the delegates will use the LRU replacement policy to remove some cached verification information to meet the storage limitation. However, when the cache ability of the delegate reaches 90%, the storage space is not a constraint, because

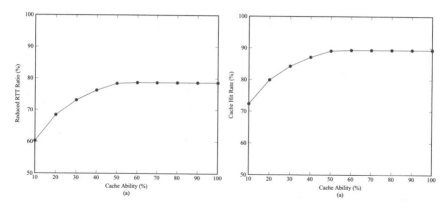

Fig. 4.9 Effects of delegate cache ability: **a** reduced RTT ratio and **b** cache hit rate

the cached verification information will be invalid (expired) before being deleted for new entries.

4.7.5 Effects of the Request Rate

In this section, we evaluate the impact of changes in the request rate on the architecture. In the evaluation, the unit of the request rate is the number of contents requested by each user per second. The purpose of evaluating the request rate is to measure the impact of the frequency of user requests on the architecture. We refer to a related study to set the range of request rates [23]. Table 4.9 shows detailed parameters. Figure 4.10 depicts the reduced RTT ratio and the cache hit rate against the varying request rates of each requester from 25 to 150.

Table 4.8 The parameters in the evaluation of the delegate cache ability

Parameter	Value
Number of requesters	345
Link delay between D_S and D_L	30 ms
Number of content	100,000
Cache size in delegates	***Change from 10,000, 20,000, 30,000, 40,000, 50,000, 60,000, 70,000, 80,000, 90,000 to 100,000***
Expiration time of verification information	30 s
The request rate	100 requests/s
Zipf (q, α)	(0, 1.0)

Table 4.9 The parameters in the evaluation of the request rate

Parameter	Value
Number of requesters	345
Link delay between D_S and D_L	30 ms
Number of content	100,000
Cache size in delegates	100,000
Expiration time of verification information	30 s
The request rate	*Change from 25, 50, 75, 100, 125, to 150*
Zipf (q, α)	(0, 1.0)

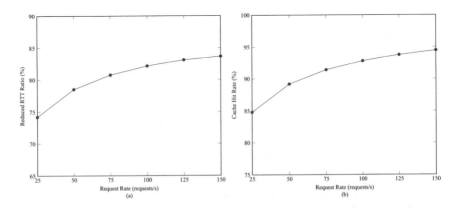

Fig. 4.10 Effects of request rate of requesters: **a** reduced RTT ratio and **b** cache hit rate

From Fig. 4.10 we observe that when the request rate increases, the efficiency and advantage of our architecture is more obvious. Specifically, when the request rate is 25 requests/s, the reduced RTT ratio is 74.20%, and the cache hit rate is 84.80%. If the request rate increases to 150 requests/s, the reduced RTT ratio increases to 83.66%, and the cache hit rate reaches 94.47%. In addition, with the request rate increases, the performance improvement will stabilize (i.e., the growth becomes slower), because the more frequently users request content, the more verifications that will be done in the local delegate. In reality, with the rapid development of the Internet, the frequency of users requesting content also rapidly increases [6].

4.7.6   Effects of the Number of Requesters

To evaluate the impact of the number of requesters (users who use the APCN architecture to request content), in this section we randomly select some users from all 345 nodes (leaf routers in the CSTNET) acting as active clients to request contents. At the same time, the other users do not request content temporarily. This will ensure that

Table 4.10 The parameters in the evaluation of the number of requesters

Parameter	Value
Number of requesters	**34, 86, 172, 259 and 345**
Link delay between D_S and D_L	30 ms
Number of content	100,000
Cache size in delegates	100,000
Expiration time of verification information	30 s
The request rate	100 requests/s
Zipf (q, α)	(0, 1.0)

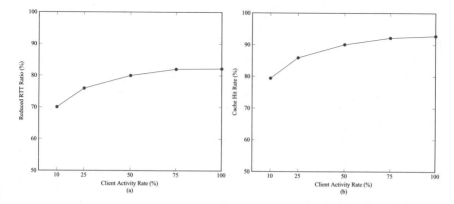

Fig. 4.11 Effects of the number of requesters: **a** reduced RTT and **b** cache hit rate

we can do this assessment without changing the network topology (i.e., the topology of CSTNET). The number of active clients divided by the total number of users is defined as the client activity rate, i.e.,

$$Client\ Activity\ Rate = \frac{N_{requester}}{N_{user}}$$

where $N_{requester}$ represents the number of active clients, and N_{user} denotes the number of users in the network.

In this section, we randomly select 34, 86, 172, 259 and 345 active clients, representing the client activity rate as 10%, 25%, 50%, 75% and 100%, respectively (see Table 4.10 for more parameters setting). Figure 4.11 shows the performance results. The results demonstrate that in the same network topology, the more requesters using the APCN architecture, the better the proposed APCN architecture performs (compared with the PKT architecture). For example, if the client activity rate is 10%, i.e., there are only 34 nodes requesting content, the reduced RTT ratio is 70.04%, and the cache hit rate is 79.41%. When the client activity rate increases to 50%, i.e., 172 requesters in the network, the reduced RTT ratio increases to 79.96%, and the cache hit rate reaches 90.08%. This means that with the increase in the number of requesters, the performance of the proposed APCN architecture is superior to that of the PKT architecture. However, with the number of requesters continues to increase, the performance improvement of APCN slows down, i.e., the reduced RTT ratio and cache hit rate increase smoothly. This is because along with the increase in the number of requesters, more requests target new content that local requesters have not recently requested. As a result, the access to the source delegate (D_S) to obtain the verify results will increase.

4.7.7   Effects of the Distance Between D_S and D_L

In this section, we study the effect of the distance between D_S and D_L on network performance when using the APCN architecture. We change the link delay between D_S and D_L from 30 to 180 ms to represent different distances in reality. If the APCN architecture is deployed on a large scale in the network, it means that many contents need to be transmitted across network domains, regions, and even countries. Therefore, we need to know the effect of distance on the utility effect of the architecture. Table 4.11 shows the detailed parameters setting, and Fig. 4.12 depicts the performance metrics against the varying distances between D_S and D_L.

Figure 4.12a shows that with the increase in the distance, the performance improvement due to the use of APCN is more obvious since the difference of RTT between the PKT architecture and the APCN increases significantly. In addition, with the increase in the distance, the cache hit rate slightly decreases, which is shown in Fig. 4.12b. This is because if the verification information cached in the D_L expires, it will take a longer time to reacquire the verification information from the remote D_S. During this period, D_L could not provide such a verification. Thus, as the distance between delegates grows, this effect becomes more apparent. According to the evaluation results, if the link delay between the sender's accountability domain and the requester's accountability domain is set to 90 ms, the RTT in APCN is reduced

Table 4.11 The parameters in the evaluation of the distance between D_S and D_L

Parameter	Value
Number of requesters	345
Link delay between D_S and D_L	*Increase from 10, 20, 30, 40, 50 to 60 ms*
Number of content	100,000
Cache size in delegates	100,000
Expiration time of verification information	30 s
The request rate	100 requests/s
Zipf (q, α)	(0, 1.0)

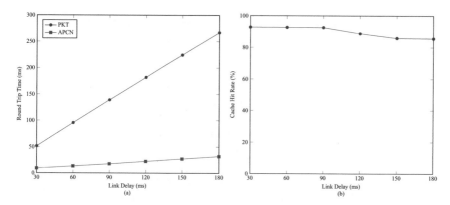

Fig. 4.12 Effects of different distances between D_S and D_L: **a** RTT and **b** cache hit rate

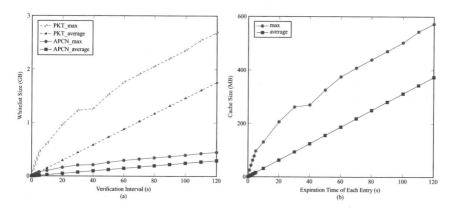

Fig. 4.13 **a** Effects of whitelist size in PKT and APCN, and **b** effects of cache size in D_L

by 87.37% compared with that in the PKT architecture. At the same time, 92.58% verification requests will be performed at the local delegate in the local network.

4.7.8 Effects of the Whitelist Size and Cache Size

We collect the network data from a border router of CSTNET to investigate the performance of the APCN architecture and compare it with the PKT architecture. This two-hour trace was taken on August 13, 2013, from 12:00 to 14:00. The dataset contains 943.55 million flows.

For the sake of comparing with the PKT architecture, in this section, we assume one flow transmits one content in the network [26]. This consideration reflects the worst case on the overhead of the proposed APCN and the general case of the PKT architecture, i.e., different flows generate different verification information. In realistic scenarios multiple flows may transmit the same content. For this common scenario where multiple flows transmitting the same content, different verification information will be generated in PKT, and it only needs to be generated once in APCN architecture.

In addition, because both the PKT architecture and the APCN generate finger-prints based on packets, this consideration makes the cost of storage and bandwidth consumption in the brief process the same. Recall that each ID (e.g., CID) is 20 bytes since SHA-1 (Secure Hash Algorithm 1) produces 20-byte digests [27]. The proposed APCN only needs to record the CID in the whitelist, but the PKT architecture needs to record two addresses, i.e., the destination address and accountability address (120 bytes) [11]. Thus, the whitelist used in APCN is much smaller than the whitelist in the PKT architecture. Figure 4.13a shows the storage cost of the whitelist in the PKT architecture and the APCN architecture where the whitelist size is calculated based on both the maximum and the average number of flows against the given verification interval. From Fig. 4.13a, we can find that when the verification interval is 30 s, the proposed APCN only requires 209.29 MB to store the whitelist, while the PKT architecture needs 1255.76 MB. When the interval is set to 120 s, 458 MB is sufficient to store the whitelist in APCN, but the PKT architecture requires 1.75 GB.

Caching verification information in D_L is the overhead added in APCN compared with the PKT architecture. The costs required to store the verification information in D_L will be investigated as follows. Because CID requires up to 20 bytes, and the fields for verification information and the expiration time require up to 5 bytes [28]. Therefore, we consider that each entry cached in the D_L requires 25 bytes in storage space. Figure 4.13b depicts the required cache size against the expiration time of each entry. From the figure, we find that even when the expiration time is set to 60 s, the average storage space required in a delegate to cache the verification information is 187.08 MB. If the expiration time is set to 30 s, 261.62 MB of storage space is sufficient to store all verification information.

4.8   Conclusions and Discussions

This chapter introduces a recently published study of ours about a content-based scheme (i.e., APCN architecture) that can be used to balance privacy protection and behavior accountability in large-scale content-based networks. A double-delegate paradigm has been proposed to improve the performance and alleviate the scalability issue in large-scale networks, and the newly introduced local delegate has been used for the privacy protection of requesters. Furthermore, a new content identification has been proposed to identify and trace a content. The security of the proposed APCN architecture in the real-world deployment has been analysed. The proposed APCN has been designed at the network layer, which makes it more effective than the designs at other layers.

In this chapter, a discrete-event simulator based on the NS-3 framework is developed and the real trace from an ISP is collected to validate the effectiveness and evaluate the performance of the proposed APCN. The results in the evaluation section have shown that APCN outperforms the PKT architecture in terms of lower RTT, and more verification can be completed in the local network domain under different network configurations.

It is worth noting that deployment of the APCN does not mean that all network users have to use the proposed architecture whenever they use the network. When users need to protect their privacy in content delivery scenarios, they can choose to use the APCN architecture. The proposed architecture can be installed as a protocol in routers and can be incrementally deployed. We will introduce other architectures for balancing accountability and privacy based on flow level and service level, respectively (see Chaps. 5 and 6). Users can choose different protocols such as flow-based, content-based, and service-based architectures in different scenarios. It should be noted that in the following chapters, we will not introduce the design similar to this chapter in detail. Considering the transmission of content as an important application scenario, we take the APCN architecture as an important example and introduce it in more detail in this book.

References

1. Carzaniga A, Rutherford MJ, Wolf AL (2004) A routing scheme for content-based networking. In: IEEE conference on computer communications (INFOCOM). IEEE, pp 918–928
2. Fayazbakhsh SK, Lin Y, Tootoonchian A, Ghodsi A, Koponen T, Maggs B, Ng K, Sekar V, Shenker S (2013) Less pain, most of the gain: incrementally deployable ICN. In: Proceedings of the ACM SIGCOMM conference (SIGCOMM). ACM, pp 147–158
3. Ahlgren B, Dannewitz C, Imbrenda C, Kutscher D, Ohlman B (2012) A survey of information-centric networking. IEEE Commun Mag 50(7):26–36
4. Majumder A, Shrivastava N, Rastogi R, Srinivasan A (2009) Scalable content-based routing in pub/sub systems. In: IEEE conference on computer communications (INFOCOM). IEEE, pp 567–575
5. Ma Y, Wu Y, Li J, Ge J (2020) APCN: a scalable architecture for balancing accountability and privacy in large-scale content-based networks. Inf Sci 527:511–532
6. Cisco (2019) Cisco visual networking index: Forecast and trends, 2017–2022 white paper
7. Dai HN, Wong RCW, Wang H (2017) On capacity and delay of multichannel wireless networks with infrastructure support. IEEE Trans Veh Technol 66(2):1589–1604
8. Fred SB, Bonald T, Proutiere A, Régnié G, Roberts JW (2001) Statistical bandwidth sharing: a study of congestion at flow level. In: Proceedings of the conference on applications, technologies, architectures, and protocols for computer communications (SIGCOMM). ACM, pp 111–122
9. Xylomenos G, Ververidis CN, Siris VA, Fotiou N, Tsilopoulos C, Vasilakos X, Katsaros KV, Polyzos GC (2013) A survey of information-centric networking research. IEEE Commun Surv Tutor 16(2):1024–1049
10. Sevilla S, Garcia-Luna-Aceves J (2015) Freeing the IP internet architecture from fixed IP addresses. In: IEEE international conference on network protocols (ICNP). IEEE, pp 345–355
11. Naylor D, Mukerjee MK, Steenkiste P (2014) Balancing accountability and privacy in the network. In: Proceedings of the ACM SIGCOMM conference (SIGCOMM). ACM, pp 75–86

12. Han D, Anand A, Dogar F, Li B, Lim H, Machado M, Mukundan A, Wu W, Akella A, Andersen DG et al (2012) XIA: Efficient support for evolvable internetworking. In: Proceedings of the USENIX symposium on networked systems design and implementation (NSDI). USENIX, pp 309–322

13. Venkataramani A, Kurose JF, Raychaudhuri D, Nagaraja K, Mao M, Banerjee S (2014) Mobilityfirst: a mobility-centric and trustworthy Internet architecture. ACM SIGCOMM Comput Commun Rev 44(3):74–80

14. Ghodsi A, Koponen T, Rajahalme J, Sarolahti P, Shenker S (2011) Naming in content-oriented architectures. In: Proceedings of the ACM SIGCOMM workshop on information-centric networking. ACM, pp 1–6

15. Mazieres D, Kaminsky M, Kaashoek MF, Witchel E (1999) Separating key management from file system security. In: Proceedings of the ACM symposium on operating systems principles (SOSP). ACM, pp 124–139

16. Amante S, Carpenter B, Jiang S, Rajahalme J (2011) IPv6 Flow Label Specification. RFC 6437

17. Yang X, Wetherall D, Anderson T (2005) A DoS-limiting network architecture. In: Proceedings of the conference on applications, technologies, architectures, and protocols for computer communications (SIGCOMM). ACM, pp 241–252

18. Stoica I, Adkins D, Zhuang S, Shenker S, Surana S (2004) Internet indirection infrastructure. IEEE/ACM Trans Netw 12(2):205–218

19. Carzaniga A, Wolf AL (2003) Forwarding in a content-based network. In: Proceedings of the conference on applications, technologies, architectures, and protocols for computer communications (SIGCOMM). ACM, pp 163–174

20. Poutievski LB, Calvert KL, Griffioen JN (2007) Routing and forwarding with flexible addressing. J Commun Netw 9(4):383–393

21. Francis P, Govindan R (1994) Flexible routing and addressing for a next generation IP. In: Proceedings of the conference on communications architectures, protocols and applications (SIGCOMM), pp 116–125

22. Henderson TR, Lacage M, Riley GF, Dowell C, Kopena J (2008) Network Simulations with the ns-3 Simulator. ACM SIGCOMM Demonstr

23. Jiang X, Bi J (2014) nCDN: CDN Enhanced with NDN. In: IEEE conference on computer communications workshops (INFOCOM WKSHPS). IEEE, pp 440–445

24. Breslau L, Cao P, Fan L, Phillips G, Shenker S (1999) Web caching and Zipf-like distributions: evidence and implications. In: IEEE conference on computer communications (INFOCOM). IEEE, pp 126–134

25. Muscariello L, Carofiglio G, Gallo M (2011) Bandwidth and storage sharing performance in information centric networking. In: Proceedings of the ACM SIGCOMM workshop on information-centric networking. ACM, pp 26–31

26. Chanda A, Westphal C, Raychaudhuri D (2013) Content based traffic engineering in software defined information centric networks. In: IEEE conference on computer communications workshops (INFOCOM WKSHPS). IEEE, pp 357–362

27. Eastlake D, Hansen T (2011) US Secure Hash Algorithms (SHA and SHA-based HMAC and HKDF). RFC 6234

28. Wu L, Barker RJ, Kim MA, Ross KA (2014) Hardware partitioning for big data analytics. IEEE Micro 34(3):109–119

Chapter 5
A Flow-Based Architecture

This chapter introduces a flow-based architecture that can be used to achieve a balance between privacy protection and behavior accountability. A self-certifying identifier is proposed to efficiently identify a flow. In addition, the mechanism of the cooperation between a delegate and a registry, which we have briefly introduced in Sect. 2.3.3, is integrated into the introduction of the flow-based architecture to show the relationship between the delegate and the registry and the working process of proposed mechanism in practice.

In this chapter, the effectiveness and overhead of the proposed architecture is evaluated with the real trace collected from an ISP. The evaluation results show that our architecture can achieve better network performance in terms of reducing resource consumption, shortening response time, and improving network stability. According to our assessment, both the bandwidth usage and storage overhead in the process of transmitting and caching verifications will reduce by more than 90%.

The remainder of the chapter is organized as follows. After a brief introduction of the research background in Sect. 5.1, the application scenarios and problem description for this study is presented in Sect. 5.2. Section 5.3 describes the design of the proposed flow-based architecture. The details of the accountability process is shown in Sect. 5.4 and the security analysis in real-world deployment is shown in Sect. 5.5. Section 5.6 conducts the performance results of the proposed flow-based architecture. Finally, Sect. 5.7 draws the conclusion of this chapter.

5.1 Introduction

As we know, the characteristics of packet-level Internet traffic are notoriously complex and extremely variable [2, 3]. With the rapid growth of Internet traffic, there is a growing interest in designing high-performance network devices to perform data

---

© Portions of this chapter are reprinted from Ref. [1], with permission of IEEE.

© The Editor(s) (if applicable) and The Author(s), under exclusive license to Springer Nature Singapore Pte Ltd. 2020
Y. Ma et al., *Accountability and Privacy in Network Security*,
https://doi.org/10.1007/978-981-15-6575-5_5

processing at the flow level to achieve specific purposes (e.g., network management). For example, in some scenarios, e.g., access control and load balancing, flow-based approach has attracted more and more attention [4]. By aggregating packets that belong to the same flow, processing overhead in the system can be reduced.

According to RFC 6437 [5], a **network flow** is a sequence of packets sent from a particular source (sender) to a particular destination (receiver) that the source desires to label as a flow. The same definition has been used in Chap. 4.

At present, there is no such an architecture in the network that can protect users' privacy, and at the same time, take the accountability of malicious behaviors based on network flows. Proposing such a solution (at the flow level) is a very challenging task, because the following questions need to be considered simultaneously: (1) In addition to the destination address, a network flow usually needs to include the source address (where the data is from), which is just what the user wants to hide. (2) How to identify a network flow efficiently and accurately to make it possible to distinguish different flows. Although the sender and receiver pairing is the same, the packets of the flows might be sent at different time. (3) How to perform the accountability based on any packet belonging to the same flow. (4) The new architecture needs to be scalable for large-scale networks.

It is a challenging task to design such an architecture, which can protect the privacy of users while being able to hold malicious behaviors accountable at the flow level. This is because the following issues should be considered at the same time:

(1) The network flow is usually identified by the source address (i.e., the sender's address) and the destination address (i.e., the receiver's address). However, the source address is the information that the user wishes to hide and protect in the network for privacy protection. Therefore, we should propose a method that can mark a flow without including the user's address.

(2) When designing an identifier to identify the network flow efficiently, the identifier should be able to distinguish different flows. For example, in a common scenario, if some files (e.g., documents or movies) are sent at different times, even if the sender and receiver are the same, they still should belong to different flows.

(3) How to verify a flow based on any packet that belongs to a flow, rather than waiting to receive more packets or even the entire flow before verifying.

(4) For large-scale networks, e.g., the Internet, the proposed architecture needs to be scalable.

Considering the above needs and challenges, in this chapter, we introduce a flow-based architecture that can be used to balance privacy and accountability, and has advantages in reducing network resource consumption [1]. In summary, the main contributions of the architecture proposed in this chapter are as follows:

- A new identifier (i.e., Flow ID) is designed to effectively identify network flows. By using the newly designed flow ID, the verification information only needs to be generated for each flow, not for each packet.
- A delegate-registry cooperation scheme is proposed to reduce the risk of disclosing users' privacy. In addition to the delegate used for recording user behaviors, another

new entity called registry, used for generating, distributing and managing user identities, is designed to lower the responsibility of each delegate.

- A multi-delegate mechanism based on blockchain technology is introduced to improve the reliability of the services provided by delegates. In addition, a lightweight recording method that allows verification information to be stored in the blockchain is used as an example to introduce how to use blockchain technology in a similar architecture. The design will lower the risk of making incorrect judgement or providing malicious services by delegates.

In addition, we will introduce how to evaluate the performance of a network layer scheme using real NetFlow data in this chapter. In the evaluation section of this chapter, the real trace collected from an ISP is conducted to evaluate the efficiency and the overhead of the proposed flow-based architecture.

5.2 Application Scenarios and Problem Description

The flow-based architecture is primarily oriented to the traditional one-to-one communication mode of using the network. For example, when a person sends his information to a cloud center (e.g., registering an account or voting online), or when a person sends a file to another person, these situations belong to the one-to-one communication mode. The one-to-one communication mode is a traditional, common and basic communication mode, which has existed to the present with the birth of the network. Therefore, the flow-based architecture has universal applicability.

Security Assumption. In the flow-based architecture introduced in this chapter, we incorporate the paradigm of the registry and the delegate cooperation into the design of the architecture, and introduce how registries and delegates can collaborate to strengthen the privacy protection of users. In reality, a single third party may be honest-but-curious. This assumption has been widely used in many related studies [6–9]. In addition, the third party may be attacked and controlled by attackers. Therefore, registry is designed to reduce the risk of delegates only in the network. In the proposed architecture, the delegate does not know the user's identity information, and the registry cannot obtain the user's behavior. Whether delegate or registry is attacked or no longer trustworthy will not affect the objectives of privacy protection in this work. The coexistence of the registry and the delegate will reduce the risk of compromised third parties. More details on how they work together will be discussed in Sect. 5.3.2, and the security analysis of delegate and registry in real-world deployment can be found in Sect. 5.5.

Threat Model. In addition to being exposed to possible risks from third parties, the architecture also faces various security threats. Threats may come from the sender, the verifier, and the receiver. Specifically, the sender might attack other network nodes by sending malicious data to the receiver, or send a large number of invalid brief messages to the delegate. The verifier may send a large number of invalid or malicious verification requests to delegates. For example, when there is no flow, i.e., no flow needs to be verified, the verifier still issues a large amount of verification requests to the delegate. The receiver may attack other network nodes through issuing a large number of malicious shutoff messages. In addition, intermediate nodes (e.g., routers) may steal the ID of a flow, add it to the header of the packet, and pretend to be the data from a normal (non-malicious) sender. Therefore, security threats may appear in the brief, verify and shutoff processes. We fully consider these risks when designing the flow-based architecture and propose mechanisms to reduce the negative impact of these risks.

5.3   Overview of the Architecture

In this section, after illustrating how to generate the identifier for network flows and the address format, the design of the proposed flow-based architecture will be presented.

5.3.1   Addresses

Similar to the APCN architecture we introduced in Chap. 4, there are three types of addresses in the flow-based architecture, i.e., destination address, accountability address and return address. Table 5.1 shows the format of different addresses in the packet header.

Different from the addresses in the content-based APCN architecture, in the flow-based architecture, address is formed by Network ID (NID), Host ID (HID), Socket ID (SKTID) and Flow ID (FID). NID is used to identify a network domain, HID represents a host, SKTID is used for the host to demultiplex packets to sockets (if an application requires ports for communication) [10], and FID can be used to mark a network flow. Although NID:HID can locate to a unique host, SKTID or FID is used for finer-grained positioning in a host.

In the proposed flow-based architecture, NID, HID and SKTID are generated by the hash of public key of a network domain, a host, and a service, respectively. In addition the newly designed Flow ID (FID) is proposed to identify different flows. In the proposed flow-based architecture, the FID is also self-certifying. Its structure is shown as follows:

Table 5.1 Address types and their formats in the packet header

Address type	Format	Note
Destination address	$NID_D : HID_D : SKTID_D$	Mandatory
Accountability address	$NID_A : HID_A : FID_A$	Mandatory
Return address	$NID_R : HID_R : SKTID_R$	Optional

$$FID = H((NID_A : HID_A)\|(NID_D : HID_D)\|(TS + nonce)\|K^+_{sender})$$

where H is a cryptographically secure hash function and $\|$ stands for concatenation. *TS* represents *Timestamp*. *Timestamp* is the start time of the given flow, which is included in the FID to distinguish different flows even if both the sender and the receiver are the same. The random number *nonce* is used to prevent the sender's neighbor nodes from guessing the value of Timestamp. K^+_{sender} is the public key of the sender, which is used to distinguish different senders in the same accountability domain, i.e., they share the same accountability delegate and may send packets to the same destination accountability domain. In addition, K^+_{sender} plays an important role in the self-certifying process [11, 12].

In traditional TCP/IP network architecture, FID can be generated by:

$$FID = H((Delegate\ IP\ Address)\|(Destination\ IP\ Address)\|(TS + nonce)\|K^+_{sender})$$

In this process, K^+_{sender} is supposed to be public. For an attacker in the same accountability domain as the sender, $NID_A : HID_A$ and $NID_D : HID_D$ can also be obtained by sniffing traffic. Under this circumstance, even if an attacker knows the exact Timestamp, the FID will not be forged due to the presence of random number *nonce*. Therefore, FID is unforgeable. Compared with the definition of a network flow introduced in Sect. 5.1, we can conclude that the proposed FID can be used to efficiently and accurately identify a network flow. The proposed FID is able to distinguish different senders in the same accountability domain and mark different flows sent from the same sender according to *TS*.

5.3.2 Working Principle of the Proposed Architecture

In view of the risk that an individual third party may leak user's information, we present the delegate-registry mechanism to achieve the purpose of decentralization. Delegates and registries will work together to balance accountability and privacy in the network. We have briefly introduced the paradigm of collaborative work between delegates and registries in Sect. 2.3.3. In this section, we incorporate this paradigm into the architecture to make it more intuitive to understand how this collaborative model works.

In the proposed architecture, *accountability delegate* is an independent third party to help hide the true address of the sender and vouch for the behavior of the sender. The *registry* is responsible for generating, distributing and managing sender's identity, i.e., Client ID. Client ID is an alias of a sender that can be changed regularly. We cannot directly locate a sender via a Client ID. Correspondingly, a sender's identity shows the true identity of the sender, but the user's real identifier is usually not changed or the process of changing is complicated.

In the proposed architecture, only the registry knows the mapping between Client ID and sender's identity. Since the registry does not participate the accountability

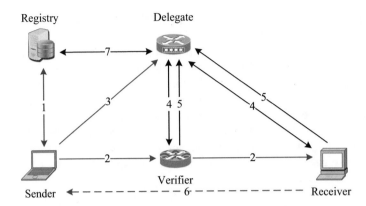

Fig. 5.1 An overview of the proposed architecture

process (see Sect. 5.4), it does not know the behavior of the sender. In this way, delegates, which possess Client ID only, will not learn the real identity of a sender, because the Client ID is only the flexible and replaceable alias of a sender. The Client ID can replace the HID in the packet header when sender sends brief messages to the delegate. Therefore, a delegate needs to cooperate with a registry to find the real identity of a sender. The registry can balance the power of the delegate. Registries will cooperate with delegates to provide (malicious) user's information under rules only when necessary.

The working principle of the proposed architecture is shown in Fig. 5.1, including the following seven steps:

1. A Sender registers its Client ID with a Registry. The Client ID can be changed regularly, but it is not necessary to have a new Client ID each time when a new transmission begins. A Sender can update its Client ID at any time, according to its preferences or actual needs. For example, the Sender believes that the old Client ID is no longer secure and may be linked to its true identity.
2. A Sender issues packets to a Receiver, using the delegate address as the source address in the packet header. In turn, intermediate nodes will not know the sender's source address. If required, sender's source address can be masked or encrypted in the payload as a return address.
3. A Sender issues a Brief message to the Delegate. The Brief message is used to verify whether the sender has sent packets to the receiver (more details on the Brief procedure will be discussed in Sect. 5.4.1).
4. A Verifier can verify whether the sender sends packets to the Receiver at any time, without waiting for all packets of a flow to be received. Any intermediate nodes between the Sender and the Receiver can act as verifiers (more details on the Verify procedure will be discussed in Sect. 5.4.2).
5. The Receiver or intermediate nodes can stop malicious flows at any time by sending a Shutoff message to the Delegate (more details on the Shutoff procedure will be discussed in Sect. 5.4.3).

6. If the sender allows the receiver to know its source address, the receiver can use the sender's source address (i.e., the return address) masked or encrypted in the payload for response.
7. When a Delegate needs to find a sender's real identity, it needs to cooperate with the Registry. The Registry should record each query sent from the delegate. If a delegate shows malicious behavior, e.g., query the information of no harmful senders or send too many query requests, we can stop the delegate's service and punish it.

In the proposed architecture, the scope of accountability domain is divided according to practical requirements, e.g., the geographical domains, business needs, or different agencies. Thus, the architecture is flexible and scalable.

5.3.3 Multi-Delegate Design

Given that the risk originating from a third party should be effectively controlled [13], if a delegate provides incorrect service, it will hinder the normal communication between sender and receiver. To address the issue that a delegate may not provide services properly, a security-enhanced design is proposed for higher security requirements, where multiple delegates are used to provide services in the same accountability domain. The purpose of multi-delegate design is to make the system decentralized. It can reduce the risk of the system, e.g., the single delegate is not trusted or cannot provide services stably. The blockchain technology [14] can be used to record Brief messages in delegates. Blockchain has been successfully applied to many sectors, such as smart contracts and e-health. The use of blockchain allows mutually distrustful parties to transact safely without trusted third parties.

For simplicity, a lightweight recording method is proposed (see Fig. 5.2). Entries (blocks) are placed according to the Timestamp. If the timestamps of different Briefs are the same, the entries are ranked according to Client ID. The first-in-first-out (FIFO) replacement policy can be used if the storage is full. Each entry contains the hash of the previous entry. A delegate compares the latest block (entry) with other delegates regularly. If the latest block is different, it indicates the data recorded is incorrect. If some delegates record different messages with other delegates, we trust the data recorded (stored) by most delegates, like the rules used in Bitcoin systems [14]. In this case, the delegate whose records are incorrect should synchronize the correct data from other delegates. When more than half of the delegates have been attacked by malicious participants, the system supported by current delegates will be less reliable (no longer secure) [14].

The lightweight and simple recording method described above is just an example. In real-world deployment, each accountability domain can adopt appropriate consensus mechanisms and deploy blockchains to record brief messages according to its own situation. The factors to be considered when selecting a consensus mechanism include, but are not limited to: the type of equipment in the network (e.g., mobile

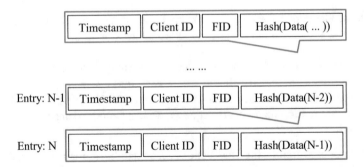

Fig. 5.2 Brief messages recording in delegates

devices with limited power or servers with sufficient power), the state of network security, and whether the network is open to the public or it belongs to a local area network in an institution.

How to choose a delegate if many delegates provide services at the same time. In the packet header, several bits can be set aside to show how many delegates in senders' accountability domain. When a verifier sends a verify message, it can choose any delegate by adding the number of delegate in the verify packets' header, or set the destination address like $NID_A : HID_A : DID_{No.n} : FID_A$, where Delegate ID (DID) is the identifier of a delegate. DID is also self-certifying and can be generated by the hash of a delegate's public key. The cost of this security-enhanced design will be evaluated in Sect. 5.6.5.

5.4   The Accountability Process

In this section, we describe the details of the brief, verify, and shutoff processes in the proposed flow-based architecture. In the following, let $\{x\}_{KEY}$ indicate a signature on x with a KEY. The KEY may be a private key or a symmetric key. For example, $\{x\}_{K_A^-}$ denotes a signature on x with A's private key and $\{x\}_{K_{AB}}$ represents a signature on x with a symmetric key shared by A and B. Let $\rightarrow$ be the packet transmission path, e.g., $A \rightarrow B$ indicates packets sent from A to B. For the sake of clarity of illustration, the following abbreviations will be used throughout this section: D_S stands for the delegate in sender's accountability domain, S denotes the sender, R represents the receiver, V indicates Verifier, P is the packet and P_{header} is the header of the packet, F represents the network flow, H is the cryptographically secured hash function, and MAC denotes the message authentication code.

5.4.1 Send Brief Message

When a sender sends brief messages, we call it the Brief process. In the Brief process, the sender S sends brief messages to D_S to notify that it is communicating with someone. Considering that delegates do not know what is included in the packet, therefore, brief messages need to contain enough information to make D_S be able to respond to any verification request according to the brief messages sent by the sender. Each brief message includes a Client ID, an FID, a Timestamp and an MAC using the K_{SD_S}:

$$\text{Brief}(F) = ClientID\|FID\|(TS + nonce)$$
$$\|MAC_{K_{SD_S}}(ClientID\|FID\|(TS + nonce))$$

In a brief message, the Client ID is registered with the registry, as described in Sect. 5.3.2. FID was introduced in Sect. 5.3.1. Timestamp has three functions. First, delegates can easily record and search brief messages by Timestamp. Second, Timestamp can be used to check whether an FID is forged in verify process (see Sect. 5.4.2). Third, if the delegate uses the blockchain technology to record brief messages, Timestamp is also essential. In the proposed architecture, a sender only needs to send one brief per flow.

If a sender is malicious, e.g., sending lots of useless brief messages, delegates can stop providing service to the sender and punish it. This behavior can be observed. For example, a delegate receives lots of brief messages from a sender, but there is no verification request sent to the delegate to verify whether the sender has sent something.

5.4.2 Check User's Behavior

The process by which a verifier checks user's behavior is called the verification process. In this process, a verifier can issue a verify message to check whether there are some delegates vouching for a sender (corresponding to the sender's behavior) and whether the currently received network flow can continue to be forwarded, since the sender has been hidden. The verify message is sent to delegates. Any nodes can act as a verifier. The process can be expressed as:

$$\text{Verify}(F) = FID\|P_{header}\|MAC_{K_{Verify}}(FID\|P_{header})$$

where $MAC_{K_{Verify}}$ is included to make sure the request is what the verifier wants.

When the verification request arrives, delegates need to check two things (named the two-step checking). First, the delegate checks whether the FID exists in the delegate, and the flow has not been stopped (shutoff). Delegate then checks if the following relationships exist, i.e.,

$$H((NID_A : HID_A)\|(NID_D : HID_D)\|(TS + nonce)\|K^+_{sender}) = \text{FID}$$

If both checks pass, it means that there is a sender sending packets to a receiver, and the FID has not been tampered with or stolen. Then the delegate replies VERIFIED to the verifier, showing that this flow is vouched by some delegate even the sender is unknown by public. The reply of verify can be described as:

$$D_S \rightarrow V : \text{Result}(F) = \{VERIFIED\|\text{Verify}(F)\}_{K^-_{D_S}}$$

where $K^+_{D_S}$ / $K^-_{D_S}$ is the public/private key pair of D_S.

We can set the verification interval to adjust the frequency of verification. If a flow has just been verified, it will be added to the whitelist. After the expiration time, the verifier can send verify message again if the flow is still alive. The evaluation of the verification rate and the impact of verification interval on the whitelist size can be found in Sects. 5.6.3 and 5.6.4, respectively.

In this process, delegates can count where the verification requests come from. If a verifier sends a large number of duplicate verify messages (regardless of the verification interval) over a period of time, the delegate will temporarily stop the verification request from the malicious verifier. In addition, if a verifier sends a lot of invalid verification requests, e.g., the received verification cannot find the corresponding sender in the records, delegates will check whether the verifier is malicious or there are some malicious nodes posing as a sender in the accountability domain.

5.4.3   Stop Malicious Behavior

When a flow is considered harmful, the receiver or intermediate nodes in the transmission path can stop the malicious flow by sending shutoff messages (instructions) to delegates, which is called the shutoff process. This process can be expressed as follows:

$$V \rightarrow D_S : \text{Shutoff}(F) = FID\|P_{header}\|duration$$
$$\|MAC_{K_{victim}}(FID\|P_{header}\|duration)$$

where the *duration* is the time the victim wants the delegate to stop verifying the flows sent by the sender.

The one who sends shutoff messages will also be monitored to prevent participants from maliciously sending shutoff messages. This process is like Brief procedure introduced in Sect. 5.4.1. But the shutoff messages should be included in the brief messages. i.e.,

$$\text{Brief(shutoff)} = ClientID\|FID\|(TS + nonce)\|Shutoff(F)$$
$$\|MAC_{K_{victim}}(ClientID\|FID\|(TS + nonce)\|Shutoff(F))$$

When delegates receive shutoff messages, they will first complete the two-step checking described in Sect. 5.4.2. It is optional for the delegate to respond to the shutoff messages. Our suggestion is that if the shutoff is successful, the delegate needs to respond to the shutoff messages. Otherwise, the delegate can ignore such an instruction, or punish the one who sends the malicious shutoff messages.

5.5 Security Analysis and Countermeasures

In this section, we analyze possible security issues and their countermeasures that the proposed architecture might encounter in real-world deployment.

5.5.1 The Trustiness of Delegates

In the proposed architecture, a registry is designed to avoid delegates to readily release user privacy. Delegates are responsible for the management of user behavior only (with whom the user communicates) without knowing the user's real identity (i.e., source address). In contrast, registries maintain the user's real identity but do not learn the user behavior. Only when a delegate cooperates with a registry, it can completely learn exactly which user has communicated with whom. However, even the delegate and registry are being attacked, the attacker still cannot obtain what (packet payloads) the sender issues, as the delegate only stores user behaviors rather than the packets being sent.

5.5.2 The Trustiness of Registries

Two potential problems may occur in registries. One is leaking user privacy, and the other is that it does not cooperate when it is required to take accountability of users (e.g., intentionally providing incorrect identity of a user). In these cases, users can directly take actions, e.g., replacing and punishing the registries. A registry has to bear the consequences. It is worth noting that, even the mapping between user's real identifier and the corresponding Client ID is leaked, one never knows user behavior, unless both the registry and the used delegate are attacked successfully. Users can change their registries at any time.

5.5.3   The Security of FID

What happened if the FID of a no harmful flow is stolen by malicious senders? We have discussed why the FID is unforgeable and self-certifying in Sect. 5.3.1. Even if a sender uses the other FID (belonging to a no harmful flow) in the packet header, the fake FID will not pass the two-step checking by delegates (see Sect. 5.4.2). Therefore, malicious senders cannot disguise as other nodes successfully.

5.6   Performance Evaluation

A NetFlow data traced from a border router of China Science and Technology Network (CSTNET) is used to evaluate the cost and feasibility of the proposed flow-based architecture, whose performance is then compared with a packet-based architecture (PKT) [15]. This thirty minutes' trace was taken on June 3, 2016 from 15:10 to 15:40, containing 73,756,072 flows.

In this section, we evaluate the bandwidth requirements in the Brief process and the storage space required in the delegate used to cache these brief messages. In addition, we calculate the verification rate and whitelist size in intermediate nodes (e.g., routers and verifiers). Finally, we evaluate the cost of implementing a multi-delegate design.

5.6.1   Required Bandwidth in the Brief Process

To investigate the effect of bandwidth on Brief process, Fig. 5.3 depicts the required bandwidth for sending brief messages for both the proposed architecture and the existing packet-based architecture (represented by PKT) against the time horizon from 0 to 600 s. To make the results easier to observe, we show the results of our architecture and the PKT architecture in Fig. 5.4a and Fig. 5.4b , respectively.

From these figures (i.e., Figs. 5.3 and 5.4), we can find that the required bandwidth of our architecture is far less than that of the packet-based architecture. This is because in the proposed architecture, brief messages only need to be issued per flow. In contrast, in the packet-based architecture, senders need to issue brief messages for each packet. In the existing packet-based architecture, the momentary bandwidth requirement for sending brief messages could reach 1,293.61 Mbps. In Fig. 5.4, we can observe that the maximum required bandwidth for sending brief messages in our architecture is 17.42 Mbps. In addition, the average required bandwidth is 6.25 Mbps in our architecture against 101.37 Mbps in the packet-based architecture, reducing about 16 times.

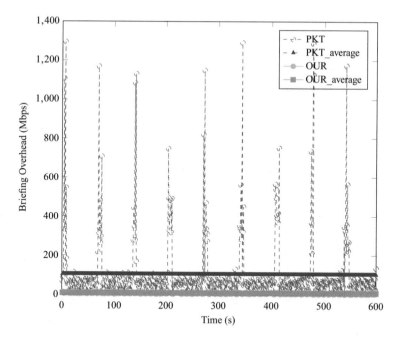

Fig. 5.3 The required bandwidth of sending brief messages

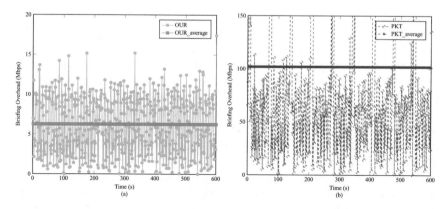

Fig. 5.4 **a** The required bandwidth of sending brief messages in our flow-based architecture, and **b** the required bandwidth of sending brief messages in packet-based architecture

5.6.2 Cache Size in Delegates

The delegate needs to cache the information used for validation. In the existing packet-based architecture, delegates need to cache the fingerprints of each packet, while in the proposed architecture delegates only require to store the FID and Timestamp for each flow. The average and maximum number of packets and flows against

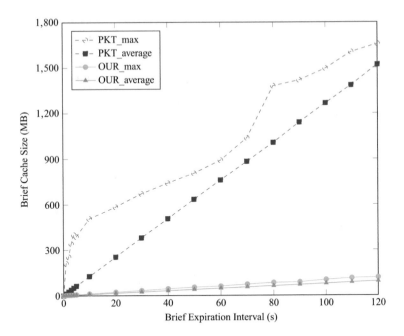

Fig. 5.5   The cache size required for storing verification information in delegates

different brief message's expiration intervals are calculated and depicted in Fig. 5.5. Since SHA-1 (Secure Hash Algorithm 1) produces 20-byte digests [16], it needs 20 bytes to store a fingerprint in the existing packet-based architecture, while in our architecture delegates need to store an FID and a Timestamp (24 bytes in total [17]) as verification information. From Fig. 5.5, we can see that the proposed architecture requires less storage space to cache verification information. The reason is that senders need to forward a brief for each single packet in the packet-based architecture, while per-flow brief messages are required in our architecture. When the valid time of verification information (i.e., brief message's expiration time) is 30 s, the average storage space of delegates in the existing packet-based architecture is 380.12 MB, while in the proposed architecture the maximum of 23.44 MB is enough, reducing nearly 16 times. When the brief expiration time is set to be 120 s, delegates in the packet-based architecture needs 1,656.05 MB (max) to meet brief storage requirements, while in the proposed architecture, 118.53 MB (max) is enough, resulting in a significant storage space reduction.

5.6.3   Verification Rate

The verification rate is calculated by analyzing the trace data. We first do the statistics on the max and average number of verified flows within a given time, i.e., the

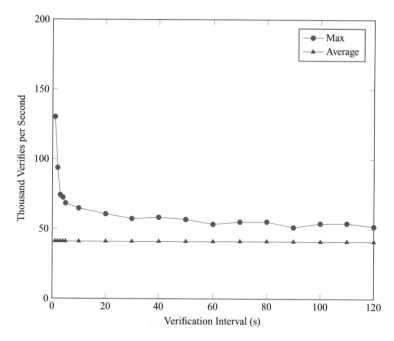

Fig. 5.6 The verification rate at delegates

verification interval. Then, we divide the interval into seconds. The result reflects the verifying pressure a delegate should withstand. Figure 5.6 shows how many verifications per second a delegate serves against verification intervals. From the figure, we can find that the pressure of a delegate is associated with the verification interval. After 20 s, with the increase in the verification interval, the maximum verification rate does not reduce significantly. This is because the impact of bursty traffic will gradually decrease along with the increase in the time interval, so that the number of verifications per second is gradually stable and is close to the average level.

5.6.4 Overhead in Intermediate Nodes (Whitelist Size)

As introduced in Sect. 5.4.2, a verifier maintains a whitelist for recording recently validated flows. In the existing packet-based architecture, a verifier records two addresses of a packet, i.e., accountability address and destination address. Each entry uses 120 bytes storage space because each address is 60 bytes [15]. In the proposed architecture, we only need to record FID. Therefore, only 20 bytes are required for each entry in the whitelist. The number of packets and flows in a given verification interval is counted, and the whitelist size is then calculated and shown in Fig. 5.7. From this figure, we can observe that if the verification interval is set to be 30 s, 32.77

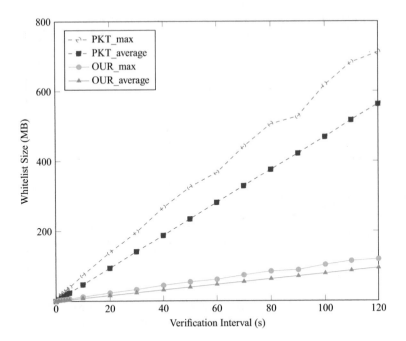

Fig. 5.7 The whitelist size in intermediate nodes

MB is enough to store all whitelist entries in the proposed flow-based architecture, while it requires 196.63 MB under the packet-based architecture. Even when the verification interval goes up to 120 s, the average size of the whitelist in the proposed architecture requires only 93.78 MB. The results show that the proposed architecture can significantly reduce the required storage space for whitelist in the intermediate nodes.

5.6.5   Overhead for Security-Enhanced Mechanism

A security-enhanced mechanism is proposed in Sect. 5.3.3 to make the system decentralized. The implementation cost of this design is analyzed in this section. In fact, the extra overhead mainly occurs in the source accountability domain. The bandwidth required for sending brief messages will increase, and the nodes need more storage for storing verification information. It should be noted that the cache size in a single delegate would not increase.

Network security has relationship with the number of delegates [14], where more delegates means more combinations. However, when we set the number of delegates, the trade-off between network security and overhead needs to be considered. Figure 5.8 depicts the overhead of bandwidth along with varying number of delegates.

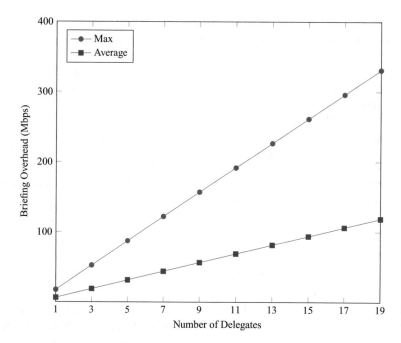

Fig. 5.8 The bandwidth of brief messages of the security-enhanced design

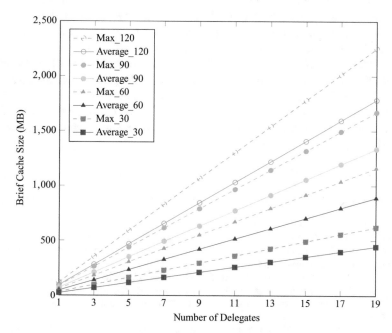

Fig. 5.9 The cache size of delegates of the security-enhanced design

From this figure, we can see that when the system has 11 delegates for recording senders' behavior, the average bandwidth required for sending brief messages is 68.77 Mbps. Even 19 delegates are involved, the maximum bandwidth usage is still no more than 330.91 Mbps, and the average bandwidth is only 118.78 Mbps. This overhead presents only in the local network, even a large dataset collected from a border router of an ISP is used for evaluation. Figure 5.9 shows the relation between the number of delegates and the cache size in all delegates with varying brief expiration intervals, i.e., 30, 60, 90 and 120 s. When the brief expiration interval is set to be 30 s, the total cache size of verification information in the 11 delegates is less than 360.48 MB. From the evaluation, it is obvious that the increased overhead (i.e., the bandwidth of brief messages and the cache size of delegates) is acceptable if the security-enhanced mechanism is deployed, and more importantly the network security has been greatly improved.

5.7   Conclusions and Discussions

This chapter introduces a new architecture that can be used to balance accountability and privacy in network layer based on network flows. A new identifier is designed to identify and distinguish different flows. To reduce the risk of disclosing user privacy, the registry has been designed to manage user's real identify and disperse the power of delegates. In this chapter, how the registry works with the delegate has been introduced, and how to improve the security and reliability of the architecture by using blockchain and multi-delegate design is discussed. Using the real NetFlow data collected, the efficiency and feasibility of the proposed architecture has been evaluated. The experimental results have shown that the proposed architecture can reduce bandwidth usage in the Brief process, and the storage overhead on delegates could be greatly reduced in comparison with the packet-based architecture. The overhead has been evaluated to be acceptable even the security-enhanced mechanism is used.

References

1. Ma Y, Wu Y, Ge J, Li J (2018) A flow-level architecture for balancing accountability and privacy. In: IEEE international conference on trust, security and privacy in computing and communications (TrustCom). IEEE, pp 984–989
2. Fred SB, Bonald T, Proutiere A, Régnié G, Roberts JW (2001) Statistical bandwidth sharing: a study of congestion at flow level. In: Proceedings of the conference on Applications, technologies, architectures, and protocols for computer communications (SIGCOMM). ACM, pp 111–122
3. Huang C, Min G, Wu Y, Ying Y, Pei K, Xiang Z (2017) Time series anomaly detection for trustworthy services in cloud computing systems. IEEE Trans Big Data

4. Qi Y, Xu B, He F, Yang B, Yu J, Li J (2007) Towards high-performance flow-level packet processing on multi-core network processors. In: Proceedings of the ACM/IEEE symposium on architecture for networking and communications systems. ACM, pp 17–26
5. Amante S, Carpenter B, Jiang S, Rajahalme J (2011) IPv6 Flow Label Specification. RFC 6437
6. Chen YR, Rezapour A, Tzeng WG (2018) Privacy-preserving ridge regression on distributed data. Inf Sci 451:34–49
7. Lai J, Mu Y, Guo F, Jiang P, Susilo W (2018) Privacy-enhanced attribute-based private information retrieval. Inf Sci 454:275–291
8. Liu C, Zhou S, Hu H, Tang Y, Guan J, Ma Y (2018) CPP: Towards comprehensive privacy preserving for query processing in information networks. Inf Sci 467:296–311
9. Shao J, Lu R, Lin X (2014) FINE: a fine-grained privacy-preserving location-based service framework for mobile devices. In: IEEE conference on computer communications (INFOCOM). IEEE, pp 244–252
10. Regnier G, Makineni S, Illikkal I, Iyer R, Minturn D, Huggahalli R, Newell D, Cline L, Foong A (2004) TCP onloading for data center servers. Computer 37(11):48–58
11. Han D, Anand A, Dogar F, Li B, Lim H, Machado M, Mukundan A, Wu W, Akella A, Andersen DG et al (2012) XIA: efficient support for evolvable internetworking. In: Proceedings of the USENIX symposium on networked systems design and implementation (NSDI). USENIX, pp 309–322
12. Venkataramani A, Kurose JF, Raychaudhuri D, Nagaraja K, Mao M, Banerjee S (2014) Mobilityfirst: a mobility-centric and trustworthy Internet architecture. ACM SIGCOMM Comput Commun Rev 44(3):74–80
13. Wang C, Chow SS, Wang Q, Ren K, Lou W (2013) Privacy-preserving public auditing for secure cloud storage. IEEE Trans Comput 62(2):362–375
14. Gervais A, Karame GO, Wüst K, Glykantzis V, Ritzdorf H, Capkun S (2016) On the security and performance of proof of work blockchains. In: Proceedings of the ACM SIGSAC conference on computer and communications security. ACM, pp 3–16 (2016)
15. Naylor D, Mukerjee MK, Steenkiste P (2014) Balancing accountability and privacy in the network. In: Proceedings of the ACM SIGCOMM conference (SIGCOMM). ACM, pp 75–86
16. Eastlake D, Hansen T (2011) US secure hash algorithms (SHA and SHA-based HMAC and HKDF). RFC 6234
17. Wu L, Barker RJ, Kim MA, Ross KA (2014) Hardware partitioning for big data analytics. IEEE Micro 34(3):109–119

Chapter 6
A Service-Based Architecture

This chapter introduces a service-based architecture that can be used to achieve a balance between privacy protection and behavior accountability. In practice, the architecture proposed in this chapter can be applied to the scenarios that belong to one-to-many communication mode, such as distributed computing. This is because in the architecture proposed in this chapter, the data packets that belong to one time or one type of services are identified by a service identifier. In application scenarios such as distributed computing, a computing task can be considered as a service and can be delivered to multiple servers for collaborative computing. In the introduction of the architecture, we take the popular Internet of Things (IoT) as one of the application scenarios to describe how to achieve the expected research goals based on services.

As we introduced in Sect. 2.3.3, in reality, a delegate can be a server, a dedicated device, or a border router that data needs to pass through. In Chaps. 4 and 5, delegates are introduced as dedicated equipment. In this chapter, we will take the service-based architecture as an example to introduce the working principle of the delegate deployed on the border routers.

The remainder of this chapter is organized as follows. After a brief introduction of the research background in Sect. 6.1, several common application scenarios as applicable examples of this architecture are presented in Sect. 6.2. Section 6.3 describes the design of the proposed service-based architecture. In Sect. 6.4, we take the IoT scenario as an example to introduce how to deploy the proposed architecture in different environments (i.e., indoor and outdoor, respectively). The analysis of the potential security issues in the real-world deployment is presented in Sect. 6.5. Section 6.6 shows the performance evaluation results of the proposed service-based architecture. Finally, Sect. 6.7 concludes this chapter.

6.1   Introduction

With the development of the Internet, in addition to the rapid growth of the number of content and network traffic, a series of diversified applications and services have also appeared in the network. Companies and service providers provide different types of services (e.g., cloud computing, cloud storage, social networking, and health management) to users. The purpose and characteristics of each application are different. The diversity of applications brings new challenges to the design of mechanisms in the network. A single architecture is difficult to apply to all scenarios.

In some (service-driven) scenarios, it is not appropriate to use content-based or flow-based approaches to achieve specific goals (e.g., balancing privacy and accountability). For example, when users use powerful computing services in the network to complete a computing task, the task might be distributed to multiple computing devices, or even distributed to multiple service providers to complete separately. The reasons for the task being sent to multiple service providers may include: users considering the costs of transmission, the price of service, and even security (e.g., users do not want one service provider to hold all the data). In these cases, if we choose to use the flow-based architecture (described in 5), a task needs to generate multiple Flow IDs (FIDs) and many verification information. This is because the flow-based architecture generates an FID per flow. This will cause a waste of network resources.

In some other cases, where the data is very large or the data will not be used many times, using the content-based architecture which has been described in Chap. 4 is not efficient. As we discussed in Chap. 4, content-based networks are often driven by requesters [3, 4], i.e., a user initiates a request for a content. However, if the data to be sent is initiated by a user (instead of being requested by other users), and the data will be sent to many receivers, the possibility of these data being forwarded multiple times is small. In other words, if we use the content-based architecture in this situation, the verification information generated based on content, including Content ID (CID) and brief messages, cannot be re-used.

Based on the above considerations, we propose a service-based architecture for balancing privacy protection and behavior accountability in this chapter. By aggregating packets and flows belonging to an identical service, the processing overhead in the system can be reduced (compared to other ways, e.g., packet-based or flow-based) [1, 2].

The term, **service**, in this chapter refers to the user requesting the service provided by a service provider, such as visiting a website for news, downloading music, or sending a task to a cloud computing center. This concept has been widely used in existing studies [5]. To efficiently identify a service, a new identifier, i.e., Service ID (SID) is proposed in this chapter. The SID is a fixed-length, location-independent name for a particular service. Each SID is mapped to a service at one time. In addition, as we introduced in Sect. 2.4, there are many advantages to implement mechanisms at the network layer. Therefore, the proposed architecture is designed as a protocol at the network layer.

In summary, the main contributions of this research are presented as follows:

- A new identifier, i.e., Service ID (SID) is designed to identify a user's behavior of connecting to the Internet and sending packets for a specific purpose. An SID can contain one flow or multiple flows. The verification information needs therefore only to be generated against each service, rather than each packet or each flow.
- We introduce the working principle when the protocol is deployed on the border router, i.e., when the delegate is located at the border of the network. This is different from the deployment location of the protocol in Chaps. 4 and 5.
- We analyze the potential issues in the real world deployment and propose the feasible solutions for different scenarios. We also analyze the security concerns of the proposed architecture.
- A real trace collected from an ISP is used to evaluate the efficiency and overhead of the architecture. The results show that the proposed architecture can efficiently provide accountable anonymous access in the network. In addition, both the bandwidth usage and storage overhead in the process of transmitting data and caching verifications in the network are acceptable.

In addition, we design a new paradigm of double-delegate (see Sect. 6.5.1), where the placement and working principle are different from those introduced in Chap. 4. The double-delegate paradigm described in this chapter is also deployed at the edge of the network (e.g., border routers).

6.2 Application Scenarios

As more and more devices are connected to the network, the Internet of Things (IoT) is formed. The IoT network has been widely used in our daily lives. IoT offers a wide variety of services (e.g., communications, data storage, cloud computing, health management, and environmental monitoring), and the IoT network is also largely driven by services [6–10]. In scenarios and applications related to the IoT, if we can identify the data packets that belong to one time or one type of service and process them based on the service, it will effectively reduce network overhead. Therefore, in this section, we take the IoT as the background and introduce several application scenarios. In this chapter, we also investigate the problem of balancing accountability and privacy in IoT networks.

We consider a simple scenario. Many families install cameras to monitor their houses. We assume that family member A is in the office and family member B is on the subway. When the camera in the house transmits video images to multiple devices (e.g., A's computer and B's smartphone), we do not want the intermediate nodes to know the house's location. Thus, what we need to do is to hide the camera's IP address when it is transmitting data. At this point, we need a solution to protect the user's identity, address and other information. This architecture should make the behavior of transmitting data to multiple end devices as a service (no matter how many flows are generated).

Let us consider another situation. In recent years, more and more appliances, such as refrigerators, air conditioners, water heaters become smart appliances, and are connected to the Internet. We can remotely control the appliance by turning it on or off via the network. When we are on the way back to home, we hope that air purifiers, water heaters, and other smart appliances to start working before we get home. If an attacker learns that we are sending such instructions to smart appliances, and knows which device the instructions come from and the IP address of the device, the attacker will then gain the user's location and estimate when the user will arrive home. Privacy protection is therefore very important in the IoT network.

According to our design, the proposed service-based architecture can be used in a variety of environments, e.g., users transmitting data using wired networks or WiFi indoors (at home or office), or users using mobile communication networks (e.g., 4G and 5G networks) outdoors. More details can be found in Sect. 6.4.

6.3 The Proposed Architecture

This section begins with an overview of the proposed architecture. Then we will illustrate how to generate the self-certifying identifier, i.e., Service ID (SID) which will be used in the service-based architecture, followed by the details of each process in the proposed architecture.

6.3.1 An Overview of the Proposed Architecture

In the proposed architecture, there are three main participants: user, delegate, and service provider (e.g., website, data center, or cloud computing center). Figure 6.1 shows the relationship between these participants in the proposed architecture.

Before the data is sent to the service provider, the user needs to interact with the delegate. The purpose of this process is mainly to prepare for data transmission. In this process, delegates will verify the authenticity and validity of the users' requests. More details on this process will be discussed in Sect. 6.3.3. After the user interacts with the delegate, it can start to issue data. When receiving the data sent by the user, the delegate replaces the source address in the packet header and hide the user's address. More details on this process will be discussed in Sect. 6.3.4. Any node that

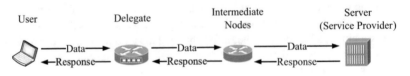

Fig. 6.1 The relationship between participants in the proposed architecture

receives the packet of the data, including delegates, servers, and intermediate nodes (e.g., routers), can challenge the validity of the data. More details on this process can be found in Sect. 6.3.5.

6.3.2 How to Generate the Service ID (SID)

When a user needs to use the service provider's servers for computing or other services, the user will generate an SID. The definitions of service and SID can be found at the beginning of this chapter. Because in the IoT network, a computing task or a request may be sent to multiple receivers (e.g., servers), an SID can correspond to multiple flows. The SID is different from the Flow ID (FID) we introduced in Chap. 5. The structure of SID is shown as follows:

$$\text{SID} = H(Timestamp \| K_{user}^{+})$$

where H is a cryptographically secure hash function and $\|$ stands for concatenation. *Timestamp* is the start time of the service request, which is included in the SID to distinguish different services from the same sender. K_{user}^{+} is the public key of the sender, which is used to distinguish different senders if they share the same delegate (K_{user}^{-} is the private key of user and controlled by the real user itself). In addition, K_{user}^{+} plays an important role in the self-certifying process [11, 12]. When a service is still going on, but the delegate receives the same SID of the service from another user (although it is unlikely to happen), the delegate will notify the later user to regenerate another SID.

In addition to the SID, we use the User ID (UID) to identify users. How to generate UID has been described in Sect. 2.3.3. If a user moves to a new location, or if the IP address of the user is changed, its UID will remain unchanged. This also conforms to the idea of ID/Locator separation, which has been considered as a trend in the future networks [11–13]. For privacy protection purposes, users can periodically change their UIDs by changing its keys (i.e., the pair of public key and privacy key).

6.3.3 Service Registration

As mentioned at the beginning of this chapter, we mainly consider that the proposed architecture (protocol) is installed on the border router in this chapter to introduce how the delegate works when it is located on the border router. In other words, the data within a network domain will be forwarded to its delegate (border router) first before being forwarded to other network domains.

It should be noted that users can choose whether to use the privacy protection function. A router that works as a delegate with this protocol deployed can forward

Fig. 6.2 The process of registration with the delegate

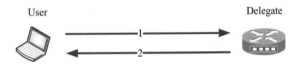

Table 6.1 The service mapping table

Service ID	User information	Service provider information
SID-1	159.226.192.***	Tencent Cloud
SID-2	UID-1	220.181.38.***
SID-3	UID-2	Amazon Web Services (AWS)
......	......	

traffic in the privacy protection mode and non-privacy protection mode at the same time, similar to the routers that can support the IPv4/IPv6 dual-stack mode.

In the proposed architecture, users need to register with delegates before transmitting data. The purpose of the registration process is to let the delegate know that the user is about to use the privacy protection service it provides. Figure 6.2 shows this registration process, which is elaborated as follows:

1. The user sends a request to the delegate to tell that it wants to use the delegate's service to hide its IP address. At the same time, the user sends the SID of the service to the delegate and informs the delegate which service provider's service it (the user) intends to use.
2. After receiving the request, the delegate will evaluate its status and whether it can provide privacy protection services for that user. If the delegate accepts the request, it will verify the authenticity of the SID. How to verify the authenticity of the SID can be found in Sect. 2.3.2. If the user's reputation is not high, or the delegate's processing and forwarding capabilities are insufficient, the delegate can refuse to provide privacy protection services. Then, the user can use other delegates in the local accountability domain to provide services.

Delegates can maintain a service mapping table to record the SID and the corresponding user information. Table 6.1 shows the main information that needs to be recorded. In addition to directly record the users' IP addresses, delegates can use UIDs to record users' information.

6.3.4 Data Transmission

After registering with the delegate, the user can start to send data. It should be noted that the packet header will always carry the SID during the data transmission process. The working principle of this process is shown in Fig. 6.3, including the following four steps:

Fig. 6.3 The processes of
data transmission

1. A user sends data to the delegate. In this step, the packet source address is the user's IP address, and the destination address is the delegate's IP address. When the delegate receives the data, it sets its own address as the source address, and the destination address is the IP address of the service provider's server. During this process, the SID in the packet header remains the same.

2. The delegate forwards data to the server. In this process, because the source address is the IP address of the delegate, the service provider will not know where the data comes from, and who is the real owner of the data.

3. The service provider responds to the user's request and returns the results to the delegate.

4. The delegate looks up the service mapping table and determines the receiver of the results according to the SID. Then, the delegate can forward the content to the user.

In the working principle mentioned above, we describe the complete process of sending and receiving data. In some cases, we only need to send data to the service provider, and only the first two steps are required.

Users can generate a set of key pairs by themselves (i.e., $K^+_{sender}/K^-_{sender}$), and then send the public key to the service provider along with the data. The service provider uses K^+_{sender} to encrypt the result which will be sent to the user who request the service. Therefore, only the user can use the private key to decrypt the content. It is worth noting that the key pair used to encrypt the data (i.e., K^+_{sender}) is different from the one (i.e., K^+_{user}) used to generate the SID mentioned above. K^+_{user} is used for authentication and can be used for long periods of time. But K^+_{sender} is generated by the user itself, and only used for data encryption. If a user uses a key pair for a long time, the service provider may analyze the user's identity based on the user's behavior. This is because if a user uses a key pair for a long time without changing it, the service provider will guess the user's identity using the received public key. In other words, when a service provider receives multiple data and they need the same public key to encrypt the result, the service provider may think that they correspond to the same source. Therefore, the user can generate key pairs periodically, and once the service provider obtains a different public key, it will not guess the user's behavior. Users can even use different key pairs for different services. Since the data and the results are encrypted by the user and the service provider, respectively, a delegate cannot know the specific content it forwards. Delegates only know that there exists a communication between the user and the receiver.

6.3.5   Verify a Service and Stop an Attack

During the transmission process, the verifier (e.g., intermediate nodes and the receiver) can challenge whether the data comes from a clear source, and the data can be verified and found if needed, to make sure the data is not an attack. The verifier can send a verify request to the delegate to ask whether the delegate has forwarded something. The process can be expressed as:

$$\text{Verify(service)} = SID \| P_{header} \| MAC_{K_{verify}}(SID \| P_{header})$$

where MAC denotes the message authentication code, and $MAC_{K_{verify}}$ is included to make sure the request is what the verifier wants. When the verify request arrives, delegates need to check two things, named two-step checking: (1) SID exists in the delegate (i.e., whether the service is present), and (2) the service has not been stopped (usually due to being reported and considered as a malicious service). If both checks pass, it means that there is a user who sends packets to the server/receiver. Then, the delegate replies VERIFIED to the verifier, showing that this service is vouched by some delegate even the sender is unknown by public.

We can set the verification interval to adjust the frequency of verification. If a service has just been verified, it can be added to the whitelist. After the expiration time, the verifier can send verify message again if the service is still alive. The evaluation of the verify rate and the impact of verification interval on the whitelist size can be found in Sect. 6.6.3.

A victim of cyber attack can stop malicious or harmful flows and the corresponding services by Shutoff. In the proposed architecture, a shutoff message is sent to delegates. Typically, receivers issue the shutoff message when they learn the flow or the service is malicious. This process is presented as follows:

$$\text{Shutoff(service)} = SID \| P_{header} \| duration \| MAC_{K_{victim}}(SID \| P_{header} \| duration)$$

where the *duration* is the time the victim wants the delegate to stop verifying the flows sent by the sender.

6.4   Analysis in Real-World Deployment

The proposed service-based architecture can be used in different scenarios. From the perspective of access, it is usually divided into two types: wired network and wireless (mobile) network. Therefore, this section will take wired networks and wireless networks as examples to show how our architecture works in different scenarios.

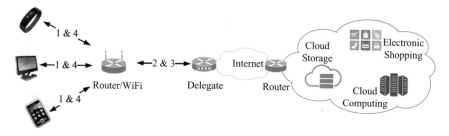

Fig. 6.4 The processes of using the proposed architecture in wired networks

6.4.1   Use the Proposed Architecture Indoors

When users connect to the network at home or office, they may use computers, laptops over wired networks, or use cell phones, wearable devices (e.g., smart bracelet) and other devices (mobile terminal) through wireless networks (e.g., WiFi). In this scenario, the router located in the user's home or office (in this section we call them home routers) serves as the first hop for the devices connecting to the delegate and the Internet. Figure 6.4 shows how users use the proposed architecture when they are indoors. The Steps (1)–(4) in Fig. 6.4 corresponds to the four steps in Fig. 6.3. More details on these steps can be found in Sect. 6.3.4.

The home router will record devices' identifiers information such as the IP address or the UID of the user and SIDs. When the device communicates with other nodes in the network, the home router, instead of the terminal device, is responsible for interacting with the delegate (e.g., providing information for verification and responding to the verification requests from delegates). This design is proposed due to the consideration of the limited power storage capacity of most mobile devices and the need of saving as much power as possible. Therefore, more interaction processes (with delegates, verifiers or other nodes) are performed by home routers which connect to power. At the same time, home routers will be responsible for the user's behavior. If a user acts maliciously, the home router should stop serving malicious users (i.e., prevent malicious users from continuing sending data), otherwise it needs to take responsibility and accept punishment. One consequence is that delegate will stop verifying all data from that home router (see Sect. 6.3.5).

6.4.2   Use the Proposed Architecture Outdoors

Figures 6.5 and 6.6 show how to use the proposed architecture when users are using mobile communication networks, such as 4G or 5G networks.

In Figs. 6.5 and 6.6, the Steps (1)–(4) also correspond to the four steps in Fig. 6.3 (see Sect. 6.3.4). In this scenario, the delegate can be located at the base station. When the base station forwards the user's data (packets), it will protect the privacy of the

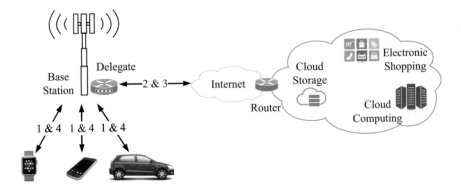

Fig. 6.5 Users use network services provided by the base station and move slowly in a network domain

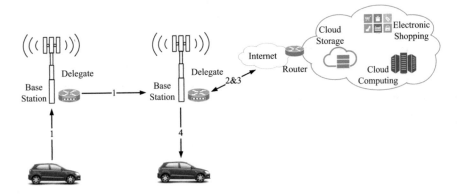

Fig. 6.6 Users use network services provided by the base station and move from one network domain to another

user and, at the same time, be responsible for the user's behavior. When an attack occurs, the delegate at the base station will stop providing services to the malicious user, thereby preventing malicious actions timely.

Figure 6.5 shows the situation when the user moves slowly. When users are moving fast (e.g., vehicles), they can choose delegates located in the incoming signal coverage area to provide services for themselves, according to their direction and speed of movement. This scenario is shown in Fig. 6.6. This approach benefits from allowing users to choose delegate on their own, which will reduce the frequency of base station switching and improve user experience.

6.5 Security Analysis and Countermeasures

In this section, we analyze potential problems to be considered in real-world deployment of the proposed service-based architecture, and their countermeasures are proposed.

6.5.1 The Trustiness of Delegates

The delegate has three basic responsibilities in the proposed architecture: (1) protecting the privacy of their users, (2) verifying the validity of the service via cached verification information, and realizing the accountability to their users, and (3) dropping invalid or malicious packets if needed.

Although delegates can be considered honest. However, what is harmful if the delegate is no longer trusted? It may release user privacy, and it may not perform verification function or may respond with incorrect verification results. Thus, they cannot take the role of accountability, and the users can decide to replace the delegate and take legal measures to punish delegates [14].

If the user (i.e., sender) and the receiver (e.g., service provider) are in different network domains, and they have different delegates, we can use a double-delegate paradigm to improve the performance of the architecture of protecting the user privacy. Figure 6.7 shows the relationship between different entities. The delegate close to the user is called the source delegate, and the one close to the service provider (i.e., destination domain) is called the destination delegate. A user can specify source delegate and destination delegate for the data transfer process.

The new proposed double-delegate paradigm in this chapter is different from the one introduced in Chap. 4 in placement and working principle. Before the data is transmitted, the user will interact with the two delegates, respectively. This process is similar to what we described in Sect. 6.3.3, but the information sent by the user is different. In this process, a user will send the SID, user IP address (or UID), and destination delegate information (e.g., IP address) to the source delegate. Meanwhile, the user will send the SID, source delegate address, and receiver address to the destination delegate. Both the source delegate and the destination delegate will record the information sent by the user.

If we use the double-delegate paradigm design in the real world, only when the two delegates (i.e., both the source delegate and the destination delegate) are attacked

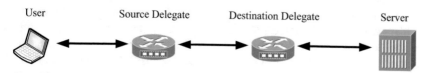

User   Source Delegate   Destination Delegate   Server

Fig. 6.7 The double-delegate paradigm

and co-operated with each other, the user's behavior could have the risk of leakage. It should be noted that, even if the delegate is attacked and discloses users' privacy (behavior), the content the user has sent will not be gained. This is because the data is encrypted during the transmission process, and the delegate cannot decrypt it (see Sect. 6.3.4). What the attacker can know is that the user has established a communication with the receiver.

6.5.2 Attacks from Users

A malicious user may send a large number of requests to the delegate that may significantly be more than necessary. The delegate can take some policies to prevent this attack, such as using bloom filters or setting a maximum number of requests received per second from the same host. This behavior can be observed. For example, a delegate receives lots of requests from a sender, but there is no data issued to the delegate.

6.5.3 Attacks from Receivers

A receiver may send a large number of invalid and malicious verify requests to delegates. If a delegate discovers that the request from a verifier is too frequent and abnormal, the delegate can drop verify requests from the verifier directly, and even punish it if the attacker is a service provider. A receiver (e.g., service provider) may attack users by providing invalid services to users or even sending malicious content to their users. If many users report a service provider's malicious behavior, delegates can tell new users about the service provider's reputation.

6.5.4 Attacks from Intermediate Nodes

Once a user successfully completes the service registration, an intermediate node (attacker) might replay any packet from that service/content to other nodes in the network. In this case, the victim will send a shutoff message to inform the delegate which SID has been used by the attacker. When subsequent packets of the malicious content (used for attack) enter the delegate, the delegates will stop forwarding them. For the attacks that occur between delegate and receivers, delegate will stop vouching for that content and the routers will stop forwarding that content, and the attack will eventually be blocked. It should be noted that, in the proposed architecture, intermediate nodes or attackers cannot use someone else's SID, and place it in the packet header of a malicious content. That is because the stolen identifier cannot pass the self-certifying. The process of self-certifying can refer to Sect. 2.3.2.

6.6 Performance Evaluation

The NetFlow date traced from a border router of China Science and Technology Network (CSTNET) is used to evaluate the cost and feasibility of the proposed service-based architecture. This thirty minutes' trace was taken on June 3, 2016 from 16:20 to 16:50, containing 1,733,581 flows.

In this section, we evaluate the cost of bandwidth during the user registration service and the storage space required by the delegate to store the service mapping table. Because in the proposed architecture we need to add the SID in the packet header, the data transmission process encounters additional overhead. Therefore, we will evaluate the increased bandwidth usage during the data transmission process in this section. In addition, the verification rate and the whitelist size in intermediate nodes (e.g., routers and verifiers) are calculated.

In this evaluation, we assume that one service contains only one flow. In other words, each flow corresponds to a service in the statistics to facilitate depicting figures [15]. This consideration reflects the worst case on the overhead of the proposed architecture. In realistic scenarios, a service may contain multiple flows because a data might be sent to different servers, which will generate many flows [16].

6.6.1 Overhead in the Registration Process

In this section, we evaluate the bandwidth required by users when they send data to delegates. We calculate how many flows per second, and then obtain the required bandwidth according to the size of each SID. Since SHA-1 (Secure Hash Algorithm 1) produces 20-byte digests, it needs 20 bytes to send an SID in the proposed architecture [17]. Figure 6.8 depicts the required bandwidth for users to send SIDs to delegates against the time horizon from 16:20 to 16:30 (i.e., 600 s). We can observe that the maximum required bandwidth for sending SIDs in our architecture is 0.98 Mbps, and the average required bandwidth is 0.15 Mbps.

In addition to the bandwidth overhead, the delegate needs to maintain the service mapping table. Figure 6.9 shows the storage space required for different service durations. If the SIDs, user information and service provider information are calculated according to the size of the self-certifying identifier (i.e., 20 bytes for each identifier), and services will last for 120 s, 7.58 MB is enough to store the service mapping table. If delegates record the IPv6 addresses of the users and the service providers, instead of their self-certifying identifiers, it only needs 6.57 MB (120 s) to record these entries, and 3.54 MB (120 s) is enough if users use IPv4 addresses.

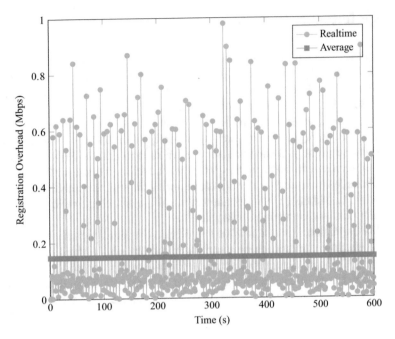

Fig. 6.8 The required bandwidth of sending brief messages in service-based architecture

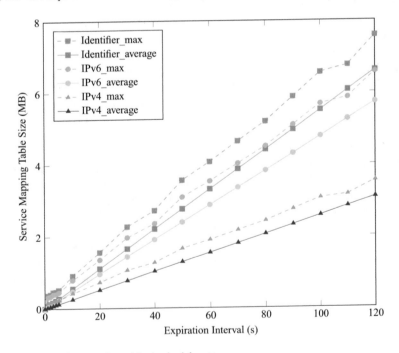

Fig. 6.9 The service mapping table size in delegate

6.6.2   Overhead in the Data Transfer Process

In the proposed architecture, we add the SID in the packet header, therefore the data transmission process requires additional overhead. We calculate the number of packets per second and then evaluate the increased bandwidth. Figure 6.10 shows the results.

To see the overhead more clearly, in Fig. 6.11 we change the value of y-axis from 0-150 Mbps to 0-10 Mbps, but the data and results used in Fig. 6.11 are the same as those in Fig. 6.10.

In Fig. 6.10, we can observe that the maximum increased bandwidth for sending data in our architecture is 121.80 Mbps. But it is just instantaneous bandwidth usage, and the dataset is collected from a border router of an ISP. In Fig. 6.11, we can observe that the average increased bandwidth is 3.98 Mbps. This overhead is acceptable in a backbone network.

6.6.3   Overhead in the Verification Process

When evaluating the overhead during the verification process, we calculate the verification rate and the size of the whitelist.

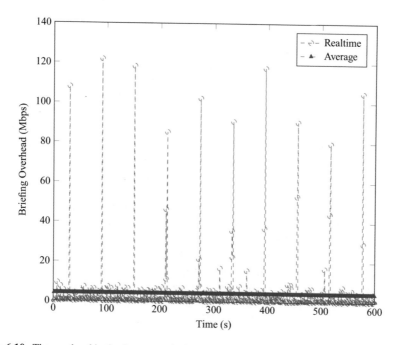

Fig. 6.10 The overhead in the data transmission process

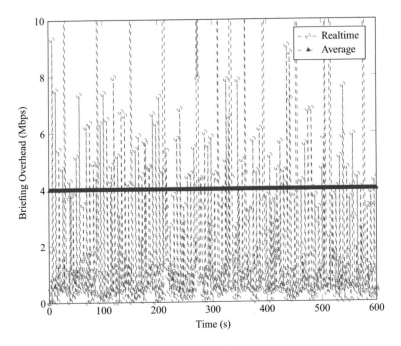

Fig. 6.11 The overhead in the data transmission process

The verification rate is calculated by analyzing the trace data. We first do the statistics on the maximum and average number of verified flows within a given time, i.e., the verification interval. Then, we divide the interval into seconds. The result reflects the verifying pressure a delegate should withstand. Figure 6.12 shows how many verifications per second delegates can serve against the verification intervals. From the figure, we can find that the pressure of a delegate is associated with the verification interval. After 20 s, with the increase in the verification interval, the maximum verification rate does not reduce significantly. This is because the impact of bursty traffic will gradually decrease along with the increase in the time interval, so that the number of verifications per second is gradually stable and is close to the average level.

As introduced in Sect. 6.3.5, a verifier maintains a whitelist for recording recently verified services. Therefore, 20 bytes (i.e., an SID) are required for each entry in the whitelist. The number of flows in a given verification interval is counted, and the whitelist size is then calculated. Figure 6.13 shows the whitelist size in the proposed service-based architecture. From this figure, we can observe that in the proposed architecture, if the verification interval is set to be 30 s, 0.76 MB is enough to store all whitelist entries. Even when the verification interval goes up to 120 s, the average size of the whitelist in the proposed architecture requires only 2.20 MB.

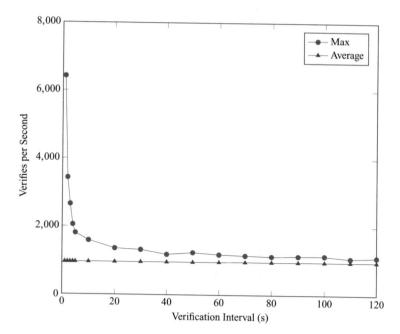

Fig. 6.12 The verification rate at users and delegates

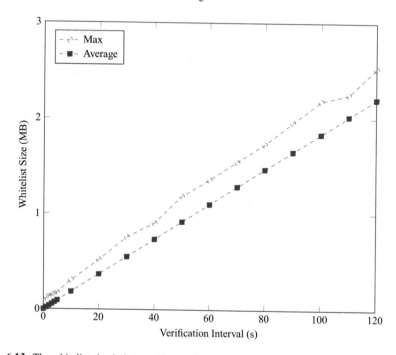

Fig. 6.13 The whitelist size in intermediate nodes

6.7 Conclusions and Discussions

This chapter introduces a service-based architecture that can balance privacy protection and behavior accountability in the scenarios that belong to the one-to-many transmission mode in the network. We take the IoT as an example to introduce the working principle of the architecture. In reality, the architecture proposed in this chapter can also be widely used in rich scenarios including distributed computing.

In the proposed service-based architecture, a new identifier, i.e., Service ID (SID) have been designed to identify and distinguish different services. In addition, the security of the architecture and the problems that the architecture may encounter in actual deployment and the corresponding solutions have been discussed. By using NetFlow data traced from a border router of CSTNET, the feasibility and cost of the proposed architecture has been evaluated. According to the analysis of the data set used in our evaluation, it has shown that the overhead of the proposed service-based architecture is small and acceptable in various processes including registering services, transmitting data, requesting verification, and stopping malicious transmission.

References

1. Ma Y, Wu Y, Ge J, Jun L (2018) An architecture for accountable anonymous access in the Internet-of-Things network. IEEE Access 6:14451–14461
2. Ma Y, Wu Y, Ge J, Li J (2017) A new architecture for anonymous use of services in distributed computing networks. In: IEEE International symposium on parallel and distributed processing with applications (ISPA). IEEE, pp 368–374
3. Ahlgren B, Dannewitz C, Imbrenda C, Kutscher D, Ohlman B (2012) A survey of information-centric networking. IEEE Commun Mag 50(7):26–36
4. Majumder A, Shrivastava N, Rastogi R, Srinivasan A (2009) Scalable content-based routing in pub/sub systems. In: IEEE Conference on computer communications (INFOCOM). IEEE, pp 567–575
5. Lee YC, Wang C, Zomaya AY, Zhou BB (2010) Profit-driven service request scheduling in clouds. In: IEEE/ACM International conference on cluster, cloud and grid computing. IEEE, pp 15–24
6. Wu Y, Huang H, Wang CX, Pan Y (2019) 5G-enabled Internet of Things. CRC Press
7. Atzori L, Iera A, Morabito G (2010) The Internet of Things: a survey. Comput Netw 54(15):2787–2805
8. Gubbi J, Buyya R, Marusic S, Palaniswami M (2013) Internet of Things (IoT): a vision, architectural elements, and future directions. Future Gener Comput Syst 29(7):1645–1660
9. Al-Fuqaha A, Guizani M, Mohammadi M, Aledhari M, Ayyash M (2015) Internet of Things: a survey on enabling technologies, protocols, and applications. IEEE Commun Surv Tutor 17(4):2347–2376
10. Zhao Z, Min G, Gao W, Wu Y, Duan H, Ni Q (2018) Deploying edge computing nodes for large-scale IoT: a diversity aware approach. IEEE Internet Things J 5(5):3606–3614
11. Han D, Anand A, Dogar F, Li B, Lim H, Machado M, Mukundan A, Wu W, Akella A, Andersen DG et al (2012) XIA: efficient support for evolvable internetworking. In: Proceedings of the USENIX symposium on networked systems design and implementation (NSDI). USENIX, pp 309–322

12. Venkataramani A, Kurose JF, Raychaudhuri D, Nagaraja K, Mao M, Banerjee S (2014) Mobilityfirst: a mobility-centric and trustworthy Internet architecture. ACM SIGCOMM Comput Commun Rev 44(3):74–80
13. Ramírez W, Masip-Bruin X, Yannuzzi M, Serral-Gracia R, Martínez A, Siddiqui MS (2014) A survey and taxonomy of ID/locator split architectures. Comput Netw 60:13–33
14. Boukerche A, Ren Y (2008) A trust-based security system for ubiquitous and pervasive computing environments. Comput Commun 31(18):4343–4351
15. Oueslati S, Roberts J, Sbihi N (2012) Flow-aware traffic control for a content-centric network. In: IEEE Conference on computer communications (INFOCOM). IEEE, pp 2417–2425
16. Kllapi H, Sitaridi E, Tsangaris MM, Ioannidis Y (2011) Schedule optimization for data processing flows on the cloud. In: Proceedings of the ACM SIGMOD international conference on management of data. ACM, pp 289–300
17. Eastlake D, Hansen T (2011) US secure hash algorithms (SHA and SHA-based HMAC and HKDF). RFC 6234

Chapter 7
An Information-Centric Networking Based Architecture

Information-Centric Networking (ICN) has become a promising candidate for future Internet architectures [1]. Named Data Networking (NDN) [2, 3] is one of the most typical ICN architectures, where communication is driven by consumers (i.e., the requester of content). A consumer puts the name of the desired content into an Interest packet and sends it to the network. Routers (i.e., nodes in the network) use this name to forward the Interest packet to the data producer. Once the Interest reaches a node that has the requested content due to in-network content caching [3, 4], the node will return a Data packet that contains both the name and the content. Consumers can therefore obtain content from any (nearby) node in the network that can provide the content. This chapter uses NDN as an example to introduce the mechanisms that can be used to balance privacy protection and behavior accountability in ICN. The introduction of the working principle and basic mechanisms of NDN can be found in Sect. 2.2. It should be noted that in this chapter, we use "user" to refer to "consumer" who uses this architecture.

The remainder of this chapter is organized as follows. Section 7.1 briefly introduces the research background. Section 7.2 describes the design of the proposed architecture. Section 7.3 shows the performance evaluation results of the proposed architecture. Finally, Sect. 7.4 concludes this chapter.

7.1 Introduction

Although the NDN architecture is designed with built-in security consideration, there are still security issues that need to be addressed, including privacy protection and behavior accountability. For example, consumer privacy information may be obtained by other nodes, and the NDN architecture lacks effective way of accountability to consumer behaviors [5, 6]. Readers are recommended to refer to Sects. 2.2.2 and

---

© Portions of this chapter are reprinted from ref. [5], with permission of IEEE.

© The Editor(s) (if applicable) and The Author(s), under exclusive license to Springer Nature Singapore Pte Ltd. 2020
Y. Ma et al., *Accountability and Privacy in Network Security*,
https://doi.org/10.1007/978-981-15-6575-5_7

2.2.3 for more discussions on privacy and accountability in NDN. Currently, there are some studies focusing on privacy protection issues or accountability of consumers' behaviors in NDN [7–10]. However, few research efforts have focused on balancing the two factors.

In the research involved in this chapter, "privacy protection" refers to protecting the user's request behavior so that the user's neighbor nodes do not know what content the user has requested or is requesting, and other nodes in the network cannot infer where the request came from after receiving the Interest packet. The "behavior accountability" means that when a network attack occurs or a user maliciously requests content, the network administrator (e.g., ISPs) can find the source of the attack within a certain period of time and hold the user accountable.

The above definitions are consistent with the definitions we introduced in Sect. 1.2. In this chapter, we will use these definitions and integrate them into the characteristics of NDN. The definitions of privacy protection and behavior accountability in this chapter are widely used in related research [5, 6, 11–13]. If the network administrator can locate malicious users in time and implement corresponding punishment measures, it will help maintain the security of the network.

In this chapter, we will introduce a new mechanism for balancing privacy protection and behavior accountability in NDN, so that users can trust and account for anonymous request content. The proposed architecture is implemented, and the network performance and overhead of this architecture are evaluated. The experimental results show that the deployment of this mechanism has lower resource overhead and lower network latency. It can effectively protect the privacy of users without affecting the user experience, and provide network administrators with the ability to hold users accountable for malicious behaviors. The main contributions of this chapter are summarized as follows:

- An architecture that enables trusted anonymous request content in NDN is introduced. This architecture not only protects the privacy of users, but also effectively restricts the user's behavior. This architecture allows NDN to prevent malicious behaviors of users in time.
- The proposed architecture has been implemented and verified, and the metrics and evaluation methods used for evaluating the performance of the architecture will be introduced. The evaluation indicators used in this research can also be adopted in related studies.

In the following sections, we will detail the design of the proposed mechanisms and how they work in NDN.

7.2   The Proposed Architecture

The architecture proposed in this chapter is designed and implemented as a network protocol. As long as the node supports this protocol, it can perform the designed steps to achieve the purpose of balancing privacy protection and behavior accountability

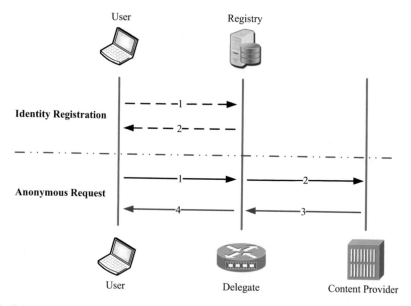

Fig. 7.1 An overview of the proposed architecture

in NDN. In the architecture proposed in this chapter, the delegate acting as an independent third party is also required to help users achieve the needs of anonymously requesting content. At the same time, the delegate can play a supervisory role. By recording the limited information of user behaviors, when a malicious behavior occurs in the network, the source of the attack (i.e., malicious node) can be found in time. We can prevent the malicious behavior from continuing and then take punitive measures against malicious nodes. For malicious nodes that cause huge losses, their legal liability can be investigated. In fact, not all requests for content need to implement this protocol. When users request popular content, they can follow the way that NDN was originally designed to request content. Users can use this mechanism for unpopular or private content.

When using this architecture in NDN, it mainly includes two processes: the process of identity registration and the process of (accountable or trusted) anonymously requesting content. Figure 7.1 shows the overview of the proposed architecture. We will introduce the two processes separately.

7.2.1 The Process of Identity Registration

Before a user requests content anonymously, it needs to complete an interaction with the "registry" to obtain its own identity identifier. We propose this design because in the original NDN architecture, there lacks of authentication for user identity. This is a reason why NDN lacks the ability of accountability for user behavior. This process does not need to be performed every time when the user requests the content (indicated by the dashed line in Fig. 7.1), unless the user decides to change its User ID (UID). This process is consistent with what we have described in Sect. 2.3.3. The difference is that this process is necessary in the proposed architecture, not an optional process. The use of registries in Chaps. 4, 5 and 6 is not a necessary process.

7.2.2 The Process of Accountable Anonymous Request Content

In the proposed architecture, a user needs to obtain the delegate's public key before issuing the Interest packet to request content. The delegate's public key will be used when the user sends the Interest packet. Due to the "public" nature of the public key, the public key of the delegate can be easily obtained without restrictions (the private key of the delegate is only known by the delegate).

In this process, we can use the Privacy Service ID (PSID) to mark requests using the proposed architecture. In addition to indicating that the user wants to use the architecture introduced in this chapter, the PSID can also represent one or more delegates that the user wishes to provide privacy services for itself. It should be noted that PSID is only a tag, and other tags can also be used. When the PSID (or other specified tags) is located in the name of the Interest packet, the Interest packet will be forwarded to the delegate. This is because other nodes do not have a delegate's private key. Therefore, they do not have the ability to handle such requests. In order words, only delegate nodes can handle such requests. If non-delegate nodes receive such requests, they will forward the requests to delegate nodes to handle.

The process when a user starts to request content is shown in Fig. 7.1. It mainly includes four steps.

1. The user issues an Interest packet. In this process, the identifier PSID is used as the name of the Interest packet (we call it Name-A). The name of the content that the user really needs to request, where we call it Name-B here, is encrypted by the public key of the delegate and is placed behind the PSID as part of the name. If Name-C is used to represent the encrypted Name-B, the name of the Interest packet in this step is in the form of *Name-A/Name-C*. Since the routing process in the NDN follows the longest prefix matching of the name [14], the Interest packet will reach the delegate by this design.

2. When the Interest packet carrying the PSID tag arrives at the delegate, the delegate uses its private key to decrypt the real name of the content (i.e., Name-B) requested by the user and encrypted by its (the delegate's) public key. Then, the delegate places Name-B in the Interest packet and sends it out. In this process, the delegate should maintain a mapping table and establish a correspondence between Name-A and Name-B. Table 7.1 shows an example of the mapping table. One Name-B may correspond to more than one Name-A.

Table 7.1 Parameters setting

Name-B	Name-A	Port(s)
/Amazon/product	PSID-1	1
	PSID-2	5
/Akamai/product	PSID-3	6
/Tencent/product	PSID-4	3
	PSID-5	2
	PSID-6	5
...	...	...

3. The Data packet carries the content requested by the user and is forwarded to the delegate. Content can be obtained from the cache or from the producer of the content.
4. The delegate determines the requester of the content according to the mapping table, and encrypts the returned content with the user's public key. Then, the encrypted content is forwarded out via the port at which the Interest packet arrives. According to the NDN routing rules, the content (Data packet) will be returned according to the path of the Interest packet and be forwarded to the user [3].

It should be noted that in Step 2, when the delegate issues an Interest packet (with Name-B as the name), the nodes in the same network domain can also receive the Interest packet. It is possible that the content is cached by a local node, but this does not affect the purpose of anonymously obtaining content, nor does it affect the effectiveness of privacy protection. In Fig. 7.1, we have not drawn/shown this meaning for brevity.

7.2.3 Location and Selection of Delegates in NDN

In this architecture, delegates can be provided by trusted third parties such as a government or an ISP. There is no special requirement on the configuration of delegates. The delegate, as a node in the NDN architecture, only needs to implement the protocol and rules of the proposed architecture. In addition, the proposed architecture allows the use of multiple delegates in a network domain to provide better services to consumers. In practical deployment, there are two main working modes regarding the selection of delegates:

1. A user chooses one of the delegates to provide services. In this mode, users can randomly select delegates, or they can select delegates they trust based on past usage history.

2. A user sends the Interest packet to multiple delegates at the same time, and then uses multiple delegates to make anonymous requests in order to obtain the content more quickly.

Delegates can be located anywhere on the network. Our recommendation is to place the delegate at the edge of the network domain, where the local network connects to other network domains. This will help the delegate get content from a wider area. The delegate itself is also an NDN node with caching capabilities. We recommend that the delegate, as the node with special functions, should have stronger caching capabilities so that more anonymous requests for content can be responded to by delegates.

7.2.4 Scale of Accountability Domain

If the accountability domain (i.e., the network area served by a delegate or a group of delegates) is set too small, the effectiveness of the proposed architecture in protecting user privacy will be affected. For example, in an extreme case, when only one node in an accountability domain recently sent a message to a delegate, and the Interest packet used to request the content is sent to the nodes located in the local network after being decrypted by the delegate, the attacker may guess which user has requested the content.

However, if the scale of an accountability domain is set too large, it may affect the performance and stability of the architecture. This is because when the delegate is executing the protocol of this architecture, it needs to consume its resources to perform the processes including encryption, decryption, query, forwarding and etc. Therefore, the larger the scale of the accountability domain is, the more users a delegate needs to serve (if the number of delegates in an accountability domain does not increase). When the requests of users in an accountability domain exceed the processing capacity of the delegate, the performance and stability of the proposed architecture will be affected. One consequence is that the time it takes for users to acquire content may increase. Therefore, we should determine the size of the accountability domain covered by one or a group of delegates according to the actual needs.

In Sect. 7.3.3, we will evaluate the effects of the number of nodes in an accountability domain based on the proposed architecture.

7.2.5 Support for Mobility

Compared with the original routing strategy of NDN, the proposed architecture performs better for mobility scenarios. Figure 7.2 shows the situation where users use the original routing strategy in NDN to obtain content in mobility scenarios. Figure 7.3

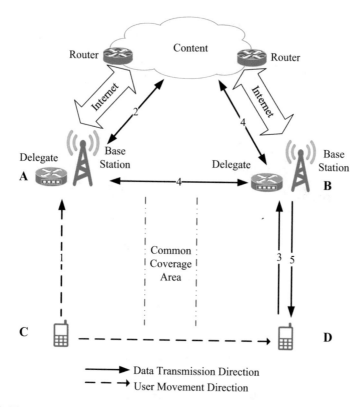

Fig. 7.2 The user uses the traditional mechanism of NDN to obtain content

depicts the use of the proposed architecture in mobile scenarios in NDN. Among them, we introduce the situation when users are located in the coverage area of multiple base stations, and Fig. 7.4 is the situation when users move across base stations. In these three figures, the solid line represents the data transmission, the arrow represents the data transmission direction, and the numbers represent the execution order of processes. The dotted line in the figure represents the direction of the user's movement. In addition, if there is a "lock" next to a line, it means that the name used in that step is not the real name (i.e., Name-B) of the requested content. For the sake of clarity of introducing the architecture in this section, we assume that the delegate is deployed in a base station.

In the mobile scenario, if the traditional mechanism of NDN is used, the situation shown in Fig. 7.2 will occur. That is, after the user moves from position C to position D, the user needs to resend the Interest packet to the surrounding nodes. If the base station B does not cache the content, the best case at this time is that the base station B obtains the content from the base station A and then forwards the content to the user. This will make Step 1 and Step 2 in Fig. 7.2 become two wasteful processes, and it will affect the efficiency of users requesting content in the mobile network.

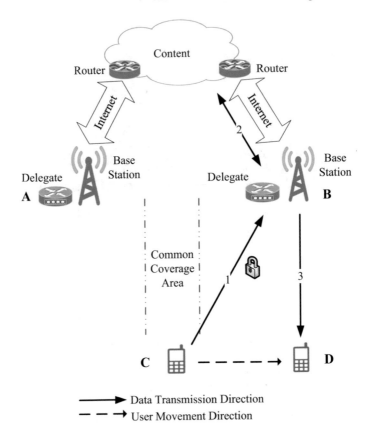

Fig. 7.3 The user is located in the area covered by multiple base stations

Figure 7.3 shows a scenario where the user is located between two base stations and the signals of these two base stations has some overlap. The user will select the delegate in the base stations that they are constantly approaching to provide services. In other words, the user selects a delegate according to the direction of movement. For example, when a user is located at position C, the name of the content that the user wishes to request in a privacy protection manner will be encrypted and be sent to the delegate which is located at the base station B. After the delegate decrypts the name, the name of the content will be sent to other nodes. Therefore, when the user moves from the position C to the position D, the user can receive the content returned from the base station B.

Figure 7.4 depicts that the user is still in the area covered by the signal of base station A and cannot receive the signal from base station B. In this case, the user sends a request to the delegate located at the base station A, and attaches his movement information (such as the speed and direction of movement). Base station A will predict the base station coverage area from which the user will receive content based

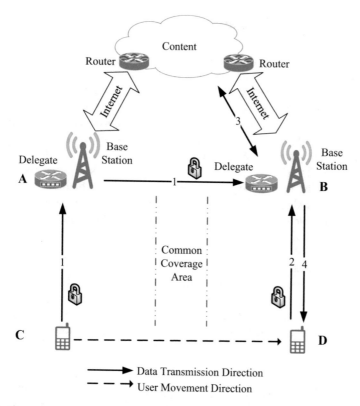

Fig. 7.4 The user moves from one area to another that is covered by different base stations

on the user's movement information. Here, we assume that the user will move to base station B. At this time, the delegate located at base station A will forward the request to base station B, and the Interest packet carrying the real name of the content will be forwarded from the base station B to the surrounding nodes. After the user moves from position C to position D, the user uses the anonymous request method to request content again. Since the content has been cached at base station B by the previous request, the content will be directly sent from base station B to the user located at position D.

Through the above-listed scenarios, we can find that the proposed architecture can be well applied to mobile communication scenarios in NDN. When compared with the traditional NDN mechanism, this architecture has better performance. This is because delegates can be selected in our architecture, which means that the forwarding path of the Interest packet can be selected to some extent, which will also affect the path of the returned Data packet.

7.3   Performance Evaluation

This section will evaluate the impact on the performance if consumers/users use the proposed architecture in NDN. We implement the proposed architecture in ndnSIM [15], a widely used platform for the evaluation of NDN. The topology used in this evaluation is shown in Fig. 7.5. It mainly includes an accountability domain, a delegate and a content provider (including content producers and nodes with cached content). The Barabasi-Albert (BA) model is used to generate the network topology by NetworkX [16], because it can capture the characteristics of real-world Internet topologies [17]. Table 7.2 shows the key system parameter settings in the simulation environment. When setting the parameters for the evaluation in this section, we refer to some related studies [4, 18]. In each subsection, we will list the main parameters in a smaller table and mark the changed parameters and the changes of their values. If a parameter is not listed in the tables in subsections, it means that it has not been changed, and its value can be found in Table 7.2.

The main evaluation indicators in this section include the average round-trip time (RTT) and the increased RTT ratio. These two indicators can reflect the efficiency of content acquisition when users use this architecture, and the changing trend of the efficiency. When using the privacy protection and behavior accountability services provided by this architecture, the time for users to request content may increase.

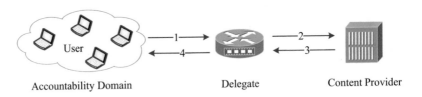

Fig. 7.5 The topology used in the evaluation

Table 7.2 The parameters setting

Parameters	Value
Number of nodes	100
Number of content	100,000
Cache size in delegates	100 packets
Expiration time of content	30 s
Forwarding strategy	Best route
Replacement strategy	Least recently used (LRU)
The request rate	30 requests/s
Link delay between producer and delegate	3 ms/hop × 10 hops = 30 ms
Zipf (q, α)	(0, 1.0)
Simulation time	300 s

However, if the increased time is short and the user experience is not greatly affected, it will prove that the adverse effects caused by using this architecture are acceptable.

The *RTT* is the time from when the user sends the Interest packet until the user receives the requested content. The *increased RTT ratio* is calculated by dividing the increased time when a user uses this architecture by the time required when user does not use the proposed architecture. The unit is percentage (%), i.e.,

$$Increased\ RTT\ Ratio = \frac{RTT_{privacy} - RTT_{normal}}{RTT_{privacy}}$$

where $RTT_{privacy}$ stands for the required RTT for requesting content using the privacy protection service provided by our architecture, and RTT_{normal} represents the required RTT when using the traditional mechanism in NDN.

In the evaluation, there are two kinds of legends, i.e., "original" and "our". The "original" represents that the users do not use the proposed architecture, and the "our" represents the use of the proposed architecture.

When we evaluate the architecture proposed in this chapter, all requests of all users are assumed to be made anonymously. However, in reality, when users request popular content or do not need to request content anonymously, they use the traditional strategy of NDN to obtain content. Only when consumers need privacy protection services, they can use this architecture to request content anonymously. Therefore, when we evaluate our architecture in this chapter, we show the efficiency of the proposed architecture in the worst cases.

7.3.1 Effects of the Expiration Time

NDN adopts a "pull" mechanism instead of a "push" mechanism to obtain content. The content producer will send the content only after the consumer issues the Interest packet to request the content. In other words, the producer will not actively send content before receiving the Interest packet. When other consumers subsequently request a certain content, the content they want to obtain may have already been cached in the network for a period of time, resulting in stale content (i.e., not the latest version of the content). Therefore, in the existing mechanism of NDN, producers are allowed to set the expiration time of content. For example, if the expiration time of content is set to 60 s, it means that the content exists in the network for only 60 s from its creation to its invalidation. After that, if consumers need to get the same content, consumers will get the content from the producer again instead of from the network cache.

In this section, we evaluate the overhead of the proposed architecture by changing the expiration time. The parameters in this section are shown in Table 7.3. As shown in Fig. 7.6a, when the other parameters are set as default values and the expiration time of content is set to 30 s, consumers wait an average of 41.69 ms to receive content according to the existing mechanism of NDN. If consumers use the proposed

Table 7.3 The parameters in the evaluation of the expiration time

Parameters	Value
Number of nodes	100
Cache size in delegates	100 packets
Expiration time of content	*Increase from 10, 20, 30, 40, 50 to 60 s*
The request rate	30 requests/s
Link delay between producer and delegate	30 ms
Zipf (q, α)	(0, 1.0)

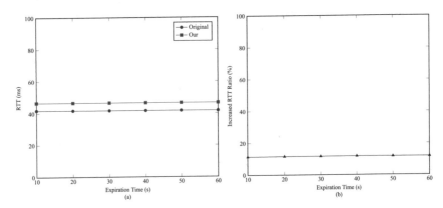

Fig. 7.6 Effects of expiration time of content: **a** average time to obtain content and **b** increased RTT ratio

architecture to request content anonymously, it will take an average of 46.54 ms to get the content. Figure 7.6b shows the growth rate of RTT compared with the original mechanism of NDN when users acquire content. It can be seen that with the extension of the cache expiration time, the increased RTT ratio does not change much and is stable. This means that even if the content expiration time is set longer, the additional time required to obtain content through the architecture proposed in this chapter will not increase significantly compared to using the existing mechanism of NDN.

7.3.2 Effects of the Cache Ability

In-network cache is the characteristic and an important component of ICN/NDN. The cache ability in the network directly affects the time and efficiency when users acquire content. In this section, we evaluate the impact of the node's cache ability on the proposed architecture by changing the size of the storage of the node in NDN.

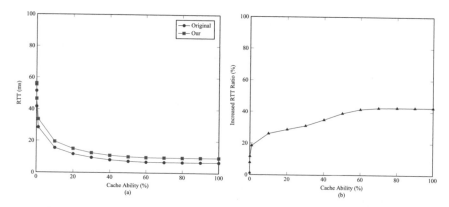

Fig. 7.7 Effects of the cache ability: **a** average time to obtain content and **b** increased RTT ratio

Table 7.4 The parameters in the evaluation of the cache ability

Parameters	Value
Number of nodes	100
Cache size in delegates	*1, 10, 100, 1,000, 10,000, 20,000, 30,000, 40,000, 50,000, 60,000, 70,000, 80,000, 90,000, and 100,000*
Expiration time of content	30 s
The request rate	30 requests/s
Link delay between producer and delegate	30 ms
Zipf (q, α)	(0, 1.0)

The cache ability is calculated by dividing the amount of content that a node can cache by the total content in the network. The results are shown in Fig. 7.7.

In the evaluation, the total number of contents is 100,000, and the number of contents that the node can cache is set to 1, 10, 100, 1,000, 10,000, 20,000, 30,000, 40,000, 50,000, 60,000, 70,000, 80,000, 90,000, and 100,000, respectively (see Table 7.4 for more parameters setting). From Fig. 7.7a, we can see that when the cache ability of nodes are gradually enhanced, the latency of using the traditional NDN mechanism to obtain content and using this architecture to anonymously obtain content are greatly reduced. When 1,000 pieces of content can be cached by each node, the average time to obtain content using the traditional method of NDN is 51.55 ms, and the average time to obtain content anonymously using the proposed architecture takes 55.59 ms. When a node can cache 10,000 contents, that is, when the node cache capacity is 10%, it takes an average of 19.50 ms to receive the content obtained by anonymous requests using this architecture. In this evaluation, when the cache ability reaches 80%, increasing the cache ability will not affect the effect of using the proposed architecture, and the time to request and obtain content in the privacy protection mode is 9.52 ms. Figure 7.7b depicts the increased RTT in detail.

Table 7.5 The parameters in the evaluation of the number of nodes

Parameters	Value
Number of nodes	*Increase from 100, 200, 300, 400, 500 to 600*
Cache size in delegates	100 packets
Expiration time of content	30 s
The request rate	30 requests/s
Link delay between producer and delegate	30 ms
Zipf (q, α)	(0, 1.0)

7.3.3 Effects of the Number of Nodes

In reality, the number of users in a network varies even within a day. For example, there are more network users in the office area during the day than at night (after work). As we discussed in Sect. 7.2.4, the number of nodes in an accountability domain will affect the privacy protection effect of this architecture, but will it affect the network performance and user experience when using this architecture? In this section, we evaluate the impact of different sizes of accountability domains and different numbers of users using the proposed architecture.

In this section, NetworkX [16] is used to randomly generate 100, 200, 300, 400, 500 and 600 nodes, respectively, as the users in the local network domain. The parameters of this evaluation are shown in Table 7.5. Figure 7.8 depicts the effect of the number of nodes (i.e., different scales of accountability domains).

Figure 7.8 shows that the number of nodes in an accountability domain has no significant impact on the traditional method of NDN and the proposed architecture. The RTT required to obtain content using the traditional method of NDN is about 41 ms, and the RTT required to anonymously request content using the architecture proposed in this chapter is about 48 ms. When the number of nodes increases, the delay basically remains unchanged. This reflects that the proposed architecture is scalable. Therefore, in the real-world deployment, we recommend to use one delegate serving more network nodes as long as the performance of the delegate allows. On the one hand, this will save the cost of purchasing and deploying delegates. On the other hand, it can better provide privacy protection services. In Sect. 7.2.4, we introduced why the larger the number of nodes in an accountability domain, the better the privacy protection effect of this architecture.

7.3.4 Effects of the Distance Between the Delegate and the Producer

In NDN, when a user requests a certain content for the first time, the Interest packet will reach the producer of the content to get the content. In addition, when the

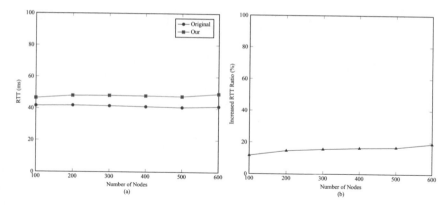

Fig. 7.8 Effects of the number of nodes: **a** average time to obtain content and **b** increased RTT ratio

content cached in the network becomes invalid (e.g., the validity period expires), or it is replaced or deleted due to the limitation of storage space, the Interest packet will also be forwarded to the content producer to request the content again. Therefore, the distance between the content producer and the delegate (or accountability domain) will also have a certain impact on the efficiency of the user's request for content. The length of the distance can be directly reflected by the link delay. We set the link delay between the delegate and the producer to 10 ms, 30 ms, 50 ms, 70 ms, and 90 ms to evaluate the impact of changes in the distance between the delegate and the producer on the architecture. Table 7.6 shows the detailed parameters setting, and the results are shown in Fig. 7.9.

As shown in Fig. 7.9, when the link delay between the delegate and the content producer is 10 ms, the average time for users to obtain content using the traditional method of NDN is 16.07 ms. The average time to anonymously request and acquire content using the proposed architecture is 18.49 ms. When the link delay is set to 90 ms, the average time for users to obtain content using conventional NDN mechanisms is 116.02 ms, and the time to obtain content in privacy protection mode using the proposed architecture is 129.11 ms. Figure 7.9 also shows that although the distance between the delegate and the producer gradually increases, the increased ratio of RTT to obtain the content is basically the same, and even decreases slightly (but the absolute value has increased). This is because the nodes between the delegate and the producer may also provide some content that has been cached. Therefore, some requests will not arrive at the producer. In practice, even if the link delay between the content producer and the delegate reaches 90 ms, the increased 13.09 ms delay in obtaining content will have a relatively small impact on user experience for most applications.

Table 7.6 The parameters in the evaluation of the distance between the delegate and the producer

Parameters	Value
Number of nodes	100
Cache size in delegates	100 packets
Expiration time of content	30 s
The request rate	30 requests/s
Link delay between producer and delegate	*Increase from 10, 20, 30, 40, 50 to 60 ms*
Zipf (q, α)	(0, 1.0)

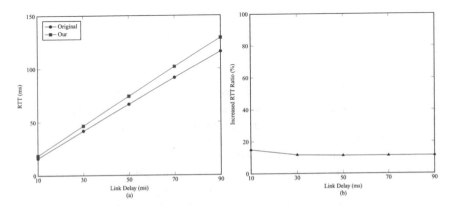

Fig. 7.9 Effects of different distances between the delegate and the producer: **a** average time to obtain content and **b** increased RTT ratio

7.3.5   Effects of the Number of Delegates

In this section, the number of users in the accountability domain is kept at 100, and then the number of delegates is adjusted to evaluate the impact of the number of delegates when users use this architecture. The results are shown in Fig. 7.10.

From Fig. 7.10, we can find that when the number of delegates increases from 1 to 11 (see Table 7.7), the time for users to obtain content will decrease, regardless of whether users request content using the traditional method of NDN or use our architecture to request content anonymously.

This is because in the evaluation, in order to maintain the consistency of the topology, we use the same topology for evaluation in different architectures (i.e., the traditional NDN architecture and our architecture). In the process of requesting content using the traditional method of NDN, the delegate has cache capability, which is equivalent to increasing the ability of the network to cache content. As a result, the delay in acquiring content using the traditional method in NDN is also reduced. For our architecture, more delegates mean that users have more opportunities to choose delegates that are closer to them to provide privacy protection services and even

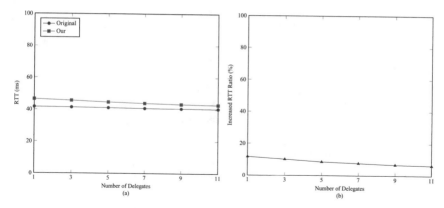

Fig. 7.10 Effects of the number of delegates: **a** average time to obtain content and **b** increased RTT
ratio

Table 7.7 The parameters in the evaluation of the number of delegates

Parameters	Value
Number of delegates	**Increase from 1, 2, 3, 4, 5, 6, 7, 8, 9, 10, to 11**
Number of nodes	100
Cache size in delegates	100 packets
Expiration time of content	30 s
The request rate	30 requests/s
Link delay between producer and delegate	30 ms
Zipf (q, α)	(0, 1.0)

the content they request (because delegate has cache capabilities). Therefore, when
using the privacy protection services provided by our architecture, as the number of
delegates increases, the time to obtain content will be reduced.

According to this conclusion, in practical deployment, we recommend to appro-
priately increase the number of delegates in a network area, which will help improve
the user experience. Users can choose an appropriate delegate based on the location
of the delegate and the quality of service the delegate provides.

7.3.6 Effects of the Consumer Usage Frequency of the Proposed Architecture

In addition to the number of users changing at different times of the day, the frequency
of users using the network also has different characteristics at different time periods.
The frequency with which users use the network can be reflected by the user's request

Table 7.8 The parameters in the evaluation of the consumer usage frequency of the proposed architecture

Parameters	Value
Number of nodes	100
Cache size in delegates	100 packets
Expiration time of content	30 s
The request rate	*Increase from 10, 20, 30, 40, 50, 60, 70, 80, to 90 s*
Link delay between producer and delegate	30 ms
Zipf (q, α)	(0, 1.0)

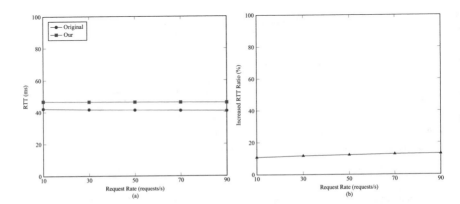

Fig. 7.11 Effects of the consumer usage frequency of the proposed architecture: **a** average time to obtain content and **b** increased RTT ratio

rate. In this section, we evaluate the impact of the frequency of requested content on the architecture by adjusting the rate at which users request content.

In this section, the user's request rate is increased from 10 requests per second to 90 requests per second (see Table 7.8). The setting of this parameter reflects how often the user uses the proposed architecture. The results are shown in Fig. 7.11. From Fig. 7.11 we can find that both RTT and increased RTT ratio are maintained at a stable level. That is, the change of the user request rate has minor effect on the user experience (no matter whether users use the proposed privacy protection service). When users request 90 times per second, it takes 40.74 ms to complete the data transfer under the traditional NDN mechanism, and 46.05 ms in privacy protection mode proposed by our architecture.

Table 7.9 The parameters in the evaluation of the content popularity

Parameters	Value
Number of nodes	100
Cache size in delegates	100 packets
Expiration time of content	30 s
The request rate	30 requests/s
Link delay between producer and delegate	30 ms
Zipf (q, α)	*(0, 0.7), (0, 0.8), (0, 0.9), (0, 1.0),* *(0, 1.1), (0, 1.2), (0, 1.3)*

7.3.7 Effects of the Content Popularity

In this section, we consider the Zipf distribution for content popularity, as it has been widely used in related studies for this purpose [19]. Some related studies show that the behavior of users when requesting content follows the Zipf distribution [4, 20, 21]. In different scenarios, the parameters of the Zipf distribution are different. We study the effect of this index on performance by changing the value of the parameter α of the Zipf distribution. The higher the value of the parameter α, the more concentrated the content requested by users. The detailed parameters setting is shown in Table 7.9 and the results are shown in Fig. 7.12. As Fig. 7.12 shows, as the value of the Zipf distribution parameter α gradually increases from 0.7 to 1.3, the time for users to obtain content has been greatly reduced. However, when using the traditional NDN mechanism, the delay is reduced faster. This is because as the content requested by users becomes more concentrated, the cache in NDN will play a greater role, and more content can be obtained from nearby nodes.

In reality, the content that users want to request in an anonymous way is usually the less popular content [22]. This is because for content that many users are requesting, the risk of leaking user privacy is small. Therefore, the content that is expected to be requested anonymously has a low popularity in the network (i.e., the value of α is relatively low), and the content is cached in fewer places in the network. In this case, the user experience when users use the proposed architecture to make anonymous requests is not much different from using NDN traditional algorithms to obtain content.

According to the results of the above evaluation, we can know that if the proposed architecture is used in NDN, while protecting the privacy of users, it will have a certain impact on the speed of users to obtain content. However, through evaluation and analysis in different scenarios, it can be found that the overhead caused by this architecture is small and the user experience does not change much. Therefore, the negative effects caused by this architecture are acceptable. It should be noted that in the evaluation of this chapter, the parameter setting reflects the worst case to the architecture, that is, all requests of all users use the privacy protection service. In reality, users can use this mechanism when they need to make anonymous requests

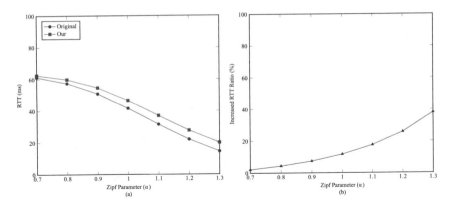

Fig. 7.12 Effects of the content popularity: **a** average time to obtain content and **b** increased RTT ratio

according to actual needs. When users request popular content, they can use the traditional NDN mechanism to obtain content.

7.4 Conclusions and Discussions

This chapter introduces an architecture that can balance privacy protection and behavior accountability in ICN. We take the representative and promising NDN architecture as an example of ICN, and introduce how to use the architecture proposed in this chapter. While protecting user privacy, the proposed architecture can ensure certain restrictions on user behavior. In this way, when a network attack event occurs, the network administrator can find malicious users in time and prevent the continuation of malicious behaviors. The evaluation results have shown that when the architecture protects user privacy, the additional overhead is small and at an acceptable level. In addition, the latency for users to obtain content when using this architecture is low, and the user experience is not greatly affected.

References

1. Ahlgren B, Dannewitz C, Imbrenda C, Kutscher D, Ohlman B (2012) A survey of information-centric networking. IEEE Commun Mag 50(7):26–36
2. Jacobson V, Smetters DK, Thornton JD, Plass MF, Briggs NH, Braynard RL (2009) Networking named content. In: Proceedings of the international conference on emerging networking experiments and technologies (CoNEXT), pp 1–12. ACM
3. Zhang L, Afanasyev A, Burke J, Jacobson V, Crowley P, Papadopoulos C, Wang L, Zhang B et al (2014) Named data networking. ACM SIGCOMM Comput Commun Rev 44(3):66–73

4. Fayazbakhsh SK, Lin Y, Tootoonchian A, Ghodsi A, Koponen T, Maggs B, Ng K, Sekar V, Shenker S (2013) Less pain, most of the gain: incrementally deployable ICN. In: Proceedings of the ACM SIGCOMM conference (SIGCOMM), pp 147–158. ACM
5. Ma Y, Wu Y, Li J, Ge J (2018) A new architecture for distributed computing in named data networking. In: IEEE international conference on high performance computing and communications (HPCC), pp 474–479. IEEE
6. Zhang X, Chang K, Xiong H, Wen Y, Shi G, Wang G (2011) Towards name-based trust and security for content-centric network. In: IEEE international conference on network protocols (ICNP), pp 1–6. IEEE
7. Lauinger T, Laoutaris N, Rodriguez P, Strufe T, Biersack E, Kirda E (2012) Privacy rsks in named data networking: what is the cost of performance? ACM SIGCOMM Comput Commun Rev 42(5):54–57
8. Acs G, Conti M, Gasti P, Ghali C, Tsudik G (2013) Cache privacy in named-data networking. In: IEEE international conference on distributed computing systems, pp 41–51. IEEE
9. Massawe EA, Du S, Zhu H (2013) A scalable and privacy-preserving named data networking architecture based on bloom filters. In: IEEE International conference on distributed computing systems workshops, pp 22–26. IEEE
10. Yu Y, Afanasyev A, Clark D, Jacobson V, Zhang L et al (2015) Schematizing trust in named data networking. In: Proceedings of the ACM conference on information-centric networking, pp 177–186. ACM
11. Chaabane A, De Cristofaro E, Kaafar MA, Uzun E (2013) Privacy in content-oriented networking: threats and countermeasures. ACM SIGCOMM Comput Commun Rev 43(3):25–33
12. Ion M, Zhang J, Schooler EM (2013) Toward content-centric privacy in ICN: attribute-based encryption and routing. In: Proceedings of the ACM SIGCOMM workshop on information-centric networking, pp 39–40. ACM
13. Ó Coileáin D, O'Mahony D (2014) SAVANT: aggregated feedback and accountability framework for named data networking. In: Proceedings of the ACM conference on information-centric networking, pp 187–188. ACM
14. Wang Y, He K, Dai H, Meng W, Jiang J, Liu B, Chen Y (2012) Scalable name lookup in NDN using effective name component encoding. In: IEEE international conference on distributed computing systems, pp 688–697. IEEE
15. Mastorakis S, Afanasyev A, Zhang L (2017) On the evolution of ndnSIM: an open-source simulator for NDN experimentation. ACM SIGCOMM Comput Commun Rev 47(3):19–33
16. Schult DA (2008) Exploring network structure, dynamics, and function using NetworkX. In: In proceedings of the python in science conference (SciPy), pp 11–15
17. Barabási AL, Albert R, Jeong H (2000) Scale-free characteristics of random networks: the topology of the world-wide web. Physica A: Stat Mech Appl 281(1–4):69–77
18. Jiang X, Bi J (2014) nCDN: CDN enhanced with NDN. In: IEEE conference on computer communications workshops (INFOCOM WKSHPS), pp 440–445. IEEE
19. Muscariello L, Carofiglio G, Gallo M (2011) Bandwidth and storage sharing performance in information centric networking. In: Proceedings of the ACM SIGCOMM workshop on information-centric networking, pp 26–31. ACM
20. Breslau L, Cao P, Fan L, Phillips G, Shenker S (1999) Web caching and Zipf-like distributions: evidence and implications. In: IEEE conference on computer communications (INFOCOM), pp 126–134. IEEE
21. Wu H, Li J, Zhi J (2015) MBP: a max-benefit probability-based caching strategy in information-centric networking. In: IEEE international conference on communications (ICC), pp 5646–5651. IEEE
22. Hummen R, Wirtz H, Ziegeldorf JH, Hiller J, Wehrle K (2013) Tailoring end-to-end IP security protocols to the internet of things. In: IEEE international conference on network protocols (ICNP), pp 1–10. IEEE

Chapter 8
Summary

Privacy protection and behavior accountability are two important factors of network security, and they are a pair of conflicting requirements. If we want to strengthen the supervision and accountability of user behaviors, it is usually difficult to avoid grasping some key identity information of users. However, identity information (e.g., IP address) is exactly what users want to hide when they use the network. Therefore, how to achieve a reasonable balance between these two factors is a challenging issue. However, most current research focuses on how to protect the privacy of users in the network, or how to achieve accountability for the behavior of users in the network. The balance between privacy and accountability is a meaningful and interesting topic that requires dedicated research.

When we decided to do the research in this area, we first investigated the problems in the current network, especially the challenges faced by privacy protection and behavior accountability. Then, we analyzed the causes of these problems, mainly from the perspective of the design of network architectures, and thought about what problems were exposed due to the evolution and the design deficiencies of the network. At the same time, we have borrowed some design ideas from the emerging network architectures (mainly from the research of future network architectures) and combined emerging network security technologies to study privacy protection and behavior accountability issues in the network.

In this book, we have introduced a general technical framework for balancing privacy protection and behavior accountability. In addition, we have proposed three basic architectures based on content, flow, and service, respectively. These three architectures can be applied in most situations to address the need of balancing privacy protection with behavior accountability. In practice, the three basic architectures can be combined to deploy in each other, and users can choose the appropriate architecture with respect to different scenarios and their needs. When designing related mechanisms, we have considered a variety of common application scenarios such as

Y. Ma et al., *Accountability and Privacy in Network Security*,
https://doi.org/10.1007/978-981-15-6575-5_8

the Internet of Things, distributed computing networks, and mobile communication networks, as well as future network architectures represented by NDN. Because of these comprehensive considerations, the architectures introduced in this book can be used in a range of common cases.

The architectures proposed in this book can be used as network layer protocols and deployed in actual networks. In Sect. 2.4, we have introduced that there are many advantages to deploying and implementing security design or security protocols at the network layer. When the architectures proposed in this book are deployed in the current network, IP addresses be replaced by the addresses that are composed of self-certifying identifiers introduced in this book.

The architectures and methods proposed in this book have been evaluated. The data collected on the routers of the China Science and Technology Network (CSTNET) have been used in evaluating the feasibility of the proposed architectures. The results have shown that the architectures proposed in this book have advantages such as low overhead, high reliability, and strong scalability.

Although we have analyzed and evaluated the proposed architectures, new problems may be exposed during the progressive deployment, which needs further exploration and investigation. In future research, it is necessary to constantly consider new requirements and propose new designs in accordance with the development and changes of the Internet. In the following, we will provide emerging issues in this topic and several potential research directions.

The challenges of new technologies. In recent years, emerging areas such as artificial intelligence (AI), big data, and data mining have brought new problems and challenges to the realization of privacy protection and behavior accountability in the network. Especially with the widespread deployment of the IoT networks and the rapid increase of the number of smart devices, sensors are appearing in every corner of our lives and collecting user data. The huge amount of data collected from users brings together, which poses a greater threat to users' privacy. In particular, the exchange and sharing of data between different organizations or companies enables users' hobbies, travels, shopping records and other information to be gathered together. Even if the user has adopted privacy protection measures in some processes when using the network, personal information such as the user's occupation, age, and even family member information may still be speculated. Therefore, while bringing higher efficiency and more powerful functions, new technologies may bring new challenges to privacy and accountability in the network.

The challenges of new application scenarios. As the needs of users in the network continue to change, an increasing number of applications require higher quality of network services. Evolving network technologies are supporting this need. We take the 5G network as an example. Users use 5G to pursue lower communication delay, which is one of the main goals of 5G networks. Although our architectures can be used in 5G networks, in order to achieve the goals of high reliability and low latency, and considering that the communication path is composed of different types of networks, we should propose a more efficient architecture, which enables the collaboration between different layers (see the discussion below).

We have several suggestions as you prepare to design a new architecture. Some research perspectives are provided below:

Cross-layer research. The network is divided into different layers. Whether in the seven-layer OSI model or in the TCP/IP protocol suite, the network layer is only a part of the entire network. We design the architecture at the network layer because of the network layer's unique advantages. In the future, when we design new architectures, we can consider all the layers of the network together. That is, different layers cooperate with each other to form a system that can not only protect user privacy, but also have a trusted relationship between users.

Cross-domain research. The *cross-domain* we are discussing here not only refers to the situation where the network is located in different regions, but also refers to the case where data is transmitted across heterogeneous networks, which may run different protocols. Let us take 5G networks as an example again. The 5G network as a new generation of mobile communication technology represents a case of heterogeneous networks. In a heterogeneous network, the network infrastructure consists of different devices and even different protocols. Therefore, many challenges need to be addressed in order to efficiently achieve the goals including privacy protection and behavior accountability in heterogeneous networks. The inconsistency of the protocols will increase the complexity of collaboration between the networks. Moreover, the missing of any one process may cause the whole design to fail.

Prospective research. Research on future network architectures is usually forward-looking. Even if it may not be deployed and used immediately, forward-looking research often solves existing problems more thoroughly, because they try to solve the problem from the basic and fundamental. By analyzing the design concept of the future networks, we can better understand the problems existing in the current network, and try to solve the problems with the methods and ideas that are not limited to the conventional network. For example, self-certifying identifiers, which have been mentioned several times in this book, can also be applied to medium access control (MAC) addresses. As we know, MAC addresses, IP addresses, and port numbers correspond to different layers of the network. This also illustrates that we need to consider collaborations between different levels of the network (as we described in the part of cross-layer research).

Interdisciplinary research. At present, the ultimate beneficiaries of the services provided by networks are end users. Whether it is rich content or powerful computing capabilities, the resources in the network are serving end users. Therefore, users are the core of the network. How to protect the privacy of users and establish credible relationships in the network can be analyzed and solved from the perspectives of psychology, sociology, and so on. The process of establishing a trust relationship between people in a real society can be mapped to this virtual society in the network. Therefore, interdisciplinary research will help researchers build an efficient architecture.

In summary, privacy protection and behavior accountability have been a long-term concern in network security. The balance between privacy and accountability is an ideal situation and is fair to every user in the network. If we can protect the privacy of users in the network and find malicious users when needed, it will help the development of the network. Although some research has been continually proposing solutions, and we have also introduced our ideas in this book, with the continuous changes in the needs of users in the network and the rapid development of network technologies, this topic (i.e., balancing privacy and accountability) will face new problems and challenges that need to be solved.

We believe that if we can take a comprehensive look at this topic from the perspective of the entire network architecture and use advanced technologies and concepts from other disciplines, the research in the area of privacy protection and behavior accountability will make new progress. More efficient, stable, reliable, and low-cost architectures will be proposed.

Printed in the United States
By Bookmasters